T0171521

Changing Vessel

Into Thine Image my Holy LORD JESUS

Kelly Bauserman

Order this book online at www.trafford.com
or email orders@trafford.com

Most Trafford titles are also available at major online book retailers.

Printed in Victoria, BC, Canada.

ISBN: 978-1-4269-2888-8

Library of Congress Control Number: 2010903995

*Our mission is to efficiently provide the world's finest, most comprehensive book publishing
service, enabling every author to experience success. To find out how to publish your book, your
way, and have it available worldwide, visit us online at www.trafford.com*

Trafford rev. 3/29/2010

 www.trafford.com

North America & international
toll-free: 1 888 232 4444 (USA & Canada)
phone: 250 383 6864 ♦ fax: 812 355 4082

Chapter 1

How does the presence of, the thought of, the *truth* that LORD JESUS is alive, affect our daily lives? How *should* it affect our daily lives? It should at the very least bring peace and joy; if one is born of the SPIRIT, the Prince of Peace inside your heart, peace and joy should almost be tangible properties that other people can partake of from you. One of my good Christian Brothers had the SPIRIT on him one day we were at church, and the peace of GOD was heavy upon him; to the point that you could see the peace present in his face and eyes; I could partake of it from him, just by talking to him. I don't think it was anything that he asked for; FATHER GOD just gave him HIS peace and my Brother was willing to share what he was given. At the time, I envied him. But since then, I have learned that kind of peace comes from knowing and walking in the WORD; our LORD JESUS; and trusting in HIM. I have since that time had people ask me what I have, and where I got it. And I gladly tell them. LORD JESUS CHRIST, my LORD.

LORD JESUS lays it on the line, with words that affect me to the core of my being:

> "He that loveth father or mother more than ME is not worthy of ME: and he that loveth son or daughter more than ME is not worthy of ME. And he that taketh not his cross, and followeth after ME, is not worthy of ME. He that findeth his life shall lose it: and he that loseth his life for MY sake shall find it. He that recieveth you recieveth ME, and he that recieveth ME recieveth HIM that sent ME."

(MATTHEW 10:37-40.)

Kelly Bauserman

Now this was LORD JESUS telling HIS disciples this when HE sent them abroad; but does it not apply to us, too? We are LORD JESUS' disciples, if we continue in HIS word, as the WORD says:

> Then said JESUS to those Jews which believed on HIM, "If you continue in MY word, *then* are ye MY disciples indeed; and you shall know the truth, and the truth shall make you free."

> (JOHN 8: 31,32.)

The point is that LORD JESUS' words even from 2000 years ago still apply, if you put them in today's perspective.

I would like to show you just how much LORD JESUS is a complete part in my life, and how this same peace and joy, and actually all of the HOLY SPIRIT's fruit, is ours to walk in and enjoy.

There should be peace and joy in our lives knowing that we are loved, and that we will never be forsaken by FATHER GOD; that all those who believe in LORD JESUS and obey GOD's WORD have an Eternal Home in Heaven. There is also peace from the promises of GOD's WORD:

> Be anxious for nothing; but in everything by prayer and supplication with thanksgiving let your requests be known unto GOD. And the peace of GOD, which passes all understanding, shall keep your hearts and minds through CHRIST JESUS.

> (PHILIPPIANS 4:6,7)

> Finally, brethren, whatsoever things are true, whatsoever things are honest, whatsoever things are just, whatsoever things are pure, whatsoever things are lovely, whatsoever things are of good report; if there be any virtue, and if there be any praise, think on these things. Those things, which you have both learned, and received, and heard, and seen in me, do; and the GOD of peace shall be with you.

> (PHILIPPIANS 4:8,9)

This, Paul said by the leading of the HOLY SPIRIT, I believe admonishing us to follow in his footsteps, for he was a man of integrity, and a man of GOD. Now days, it's very difficult to find someone worthy to imitate, therefore I think that following in LORD JESUS' footsteps on a daily, minutely basis is appropriate for our own walks. Go right to the source, for LORD JESUS *is* our source. HE prayed quite frequently, alone with HIS FATHER, I can only imagine what they talked about, but none the less, we need to have our quiet time with our Heavenly HOLY FATHER, just as LORD JESUS did.

I was just given this- just as LORD JESUS was away from Heaven, to be on this earth with us, we are away from our Heavenly Home; just as LORD JESUS needed to share the experiences of earthly life, and pray for the strength and perseverance from HIS FATHER, we also need to keep in contact with our HOLY FATHER, for the things we need to accomplish HIS HOLY perfect will in our lives here.

In addition to asking for things, I believe LORD JESUS just plain *loved* on HIS FATHER, as we need to; as we should want to, if we truly love HIM; and I know, my Brothers, and Sisters in our LORD JESUS, that you do. Tell them how much you love them, it will bless their heart. Speak in the HOLY GHOST, communing directly with FATHER and SON; it will bless *your* heart.

My LORD JESUS told me to include writing on the subject of the things we are to think upon using my personal experiences. Let's begin with things that are true; I believe that the WORD is true. Dwelling on the WORD is Scriptural, as in PSALMS 1:2:

> Blessed *is* the man that walketh not in the counsel of the ungodly, nor standeth in the way of sinners, nor sitteth in the seat of the scornful. But his delight *is* in the law of the LORD; and in HIS law doth he meditate day and night.

I am led to think about the WORD at the most amazing times, like right before Satan tempts me with sin; the HOLY SPIRIT will remind me of what the WORD says about just what is being offered by Satan. It makes me wonder, just how things are connected. FATHER GOD uses the temptations of Satan to teach me obedience, whereas before, I would give in at the drop of a hat.

Our thought process is a complicated thing; the variables being what we are exposed to; as far as memories go, what comes into our minds; our five senses, causing memories submerged to emerge, my favorite being that of smell. These exposures, including what we are currently seeing, hearing, touching, and tasting cause us to *think*; what this Word is saying, is that we need to put into practice the old adage- Garbage in, Garbage out. Or better yet, SPIRIT in, SPIRIT out; to keep this positive. If we are only listening to music which cuts down authority, or takes my LORD's Name in vain, guess what? It's probably going to set itself up as an attitude, or a pattern of thought. If one reads the WORD, even sporadically, it changes what that person's thoughts are.

If enough of the WORD is present, what a person will fall back on when there is no input, will be the WORD, for the HOLY SPIRIT will bring what you have in your repertoire (in your heart, and mind) to your thoughts. If we think upon things that are pure, like the WORD, we keep continually growing in the knowledge of the WORD, allowing the HOLY SPIRIT to use the WORD we have in our hearts and minds to keep changing us into our LORD JESUS' image, fulfilling FATHER GOD's Holy perfect will for our lives.

I am in the midst of a conflict right at the moment, between my flesh and my spirit. My spirit wants to write, my flesh wants to fantasize. Guess who will win? My flesh must die the death. The SPIRIT of my LORD JESUS is stronger than my fleshly desires. In the WORD it says the "the spirit indeed is willing, but the flesh *is* weak." (MATTHEW 26:41.)Taking the WORD at face value, the SPIRIT helps our infirmities (ROMANS 8:26), and this is the infirmity, the fight between my spirit and my flesh. For as the WORD says,

> For the flesh lusteth against the SPIRIT, and the SPIRIT against the flesh: and these are contrary the one to the other: so that you cannot do the things that you would.

> (GALATIANS 5:17.)

But I am going to do the things I am meant to do, by the HOLY perfect will of my FATHER, for I want to do what HIS WORD says to do: Walk in the SPIRIT, and you will not fulfill the lust of the flesh. (GALATIANS 5:16). I talk a good talk, but when it comes right down to it, I fell, just now, giving into the flesh. I would say it's because I haven't been solely dwelling upon the WORD lately, and it has made me weak. I have sought forgiveness, and received it, and have repented of the wicked works of my old master. I believe that every time this battle rages, a small victory is made, even though Satan wants me to believe that I have utterly failed FATHER GOD, which if you look at the circumstance, I have; but each and every time I fall to this trap, I get closer to understanding why I do these things. Therefore, I understand more what the WORD says in resisting the Devil. I just *chose* to sin; it was not forced, and it is quite unnecessary to say that complacency is my biggest enemy next to Satan, himself. I cannot let myself get to the point of saying within myself that it no longer matters what I do, because it very much does; resisting the Devil when he tries to tell me that it is a waste of time now to walk in the SPIRIT, after sinning. Remember, he *is* a liar, and the father of lies (JOHN 8:44). I must get FATHER GOD's peace back, and rest in faith again. I have prayed for GOD's Mercy and HIS Grace to be upon me again; that is the reason I have continued to write about this incident; to let you reading this that may be experiencing the same things right now, or maybe know someone who is/ has that FATHER GOD *is* merciful, and mercy rejoiceth against judgment (JAMES 2:13).

Today I had the same battle go on, and once again I chose to sin; the roots of my disobedience are like dandelion roots; they are particularly difficult to remove, because they are so deep. Even when you've pulled them up, and think you have all of it, it manages to grow back again. Praise FATHER GOD that HE is able to get the whole thing, in HIS time. I had sought and received forgiveness this morning; when praying later in the morning, I mentioned to my LORD that I asked that all prayers be continuing despite my sin that morning; HIS response was, and I quote, "What sin?" Praise HIM! Once HE forgives a sin, it is forgotten, never to be remembered again!

> As far as the east is from the west, *so* far hath HE removed our transgressions from us.
>
> (PSALMS 103:12)

> For I will be merciful to their unrighteousness, and their sins and their iniquities will I remember no more.
>
> (HEBREWS 8:12)

Dwelling on things of a pure nature, I think of FATHER GOD's and my LORD JESUS' love for each of us, love so powerful that it caused LORD JESUS to hang on that cross till HE *died*. HE died for each and every one of us.

Their love for me has been phenomenal, every time I needed, or need help, they, with their HOLY SPIRIT, are there immediately with whatever I need; from my angel's interventions, to their patient dealing with my problem sin patterns. Their love has been manifested in my many relationships over the years; most of which are still present. Some have been hard lessons in learning *to* love; other's have been lessons in who to avoid, that is those who don't want LORD JESUS as their lord; and even those I am learning to pray continually for, believing that they, too will be turned from disbelief to believing in my LORD.

A good report maketh the bones fat (PROVERBS 15:30) understand it means healthy. Things that we think upon that are of good report, like the news bulletins I receive from CBN (Christian Broadcasting Network) are very important these days, when all you hear on TV and the newspapers is evil, wickedness, and corruption. A good report can be as simple as good grades on a report card, to news of someone you have been praying for being healed, or delivered, or best of all, saved from the wrath to come.

If there be any praise, think on these things; we all know of things to praise our LORD for, from our own salvation in HIM, to HIS nearing return, which will usher us into Eternity, which I am waiting so very patiently for; to HIS gentle words of love to our hearts, minds, and souls. I praise HIM for the woman HE has chosen for me being manifested in my life; all in faith, in my LORD JESUS' Name. I praise HIM for the faith to keep going, and of course HIS magnificent Grace, and Mercy, without which I would be dead, and burning in hell right now.

Think on the good things, my fellow Brothers and Sisters; all you who are, and who will be my fellow heirs. Talk to them; tell them how much you love them. Let them tell you how much they love you; read the WORD, ingest it into your very soul; know it is LORD JESUS, HIMSELF, that you are taking in. Rejoice! And again I say, rejoice!

Chapter 2

To those that have asked LORD JESUS into their hearts, to be their LORD and KING, FATHER GOD's peace comes from having their presence in our hearts; knowing that HE is there, that HIS SON is there, and that the earnest of our inheritance-the HOLY SPIRIT, is in our hearts. I find peace in that knowledge and understanding. In faith, we believe. And after so much is opened up to us, LORD JESUS showing us FATHER GOD, it's almost like faith becomes knowledge; we *know* THEY are with us, and we believe THEY will never leave us or forsake us, for the WORD says in HEBREWS 13:5,6:

> Let *your* conversation *be* without covetousness; and *be* content with such things as you have: for HE hath said, I will never leave thee, nor forsake thee.

It is the basis for my peace. Not of this world, but Heavenly peace. Regardless of what happens to me, HIS faithfulness is one constant in this world that I count on.

FATHER GOD's peace comes from praying, and letting HIM know what you need, believing that you have received what you have asked for according to the WORD:

> Ask, and it shall be given you; seek, and ye shall find; knock, and it shall be opened unto you: for everyone that asketh, recieveth; and he that seeketh, findeth; and to him that knocketh it shall be opened. Or what man is there of you, whom if his son ask bread, will he give him a stone? Or if he ask a fish, will he give him a serpent? If ye then, being evil, know how to give good gifts to your children,

how much more shall your Heavenly FATHER give the
HOLY SPIRIT to them that ask HIM?

(MATTHEW 7:7-11.)

But let him ask in faith, nothing wavering. For he that
wavereth is like a wave of the sea driven with the wind
and tossed. For let not that man think that he shall receive
anything of the LORD. A double minded man *is* unstable
in all his ways.

(JAMES 1:6-8)

Wavering is likened to doubting that you have received. Overcome
doubt, knowing that LORD JESUS has experienced all the emotions that
are common to man, yet without sin. Remember that LORD JESUS is all
GOD, and all man; HE experienced doubt and overcame it.

I included this last verse because I have been at times double minded;
and it's true, I became very unstable until I confessed my sin of double
mindedness and sought to be single minded- straight unto my LORD
JESUS again.

It's curious, too that the verse before the one about being double-
minded has two versions, depending upon which account of the Gospel
you read; MATTHEW 7:11 says "good things" that GOD will give to
those that ask HIM; where as in the Gospel of LUKE, chapter 11 verse 13,
it states the" HOLY SPIRIT" that GOD gives. FATHER GOD may see
HIS good gifts *as being* the HOLY SPIRIT, and all the gifts of the SPIRIT
that we are allowed to walk in. That's the way I am taking it.

Also, when you think about FATHER GOD giving the HOLY
SPIRIT, when you become born of the SPIRIT, isn't it an automatic
thing that happens? The only time I asked anything concerning the HOLY
SPIRIT, was when I asked to be baptized in the HOLY GHOST. Other
than that HE entered my heart at the same time that FATHER GOD and
LORD JESUS did. THEY gave HIM to me. It is utterly my audacity that
even dares to question why the WORD says what it does. FATHER GOD
please forgive me, in THY Name, my LORD JESUS, for questioning
the giving of YOUR HOLY SPIRIT. I just wanted to know, if we had to
ask for the HOLY SPIRIT to come into our lives, or if YOU give HIM

spontaneously when we come to YOU, LORD JESUS? This knowledge would be helpful to new born again Christians.

I myself was given the HOLY SPIRIT twice, the first time when I first became a Christian back in 1982; the second time was after FATHER GOD judged me unworthy of HIS Kingdom and banished me. (See CHOSEN VESSEL, chapter 5). HE then, in HIS mighty Mercy, led me to ask for LORD JESUS to come back into my heart (which HE did), and HIS HOLY SPIRIT came back in with HIM. I have since then regained my LORD's favor, by HIS Grace and Mercy towards me (totally undeserved, I might add) and have been working on this book you are holding for nigh on 6 months (as of August 6, 2009). It has taken a lot of strength to keep going, and I want to give credit where credit is due. All that I have accomplished in the writing of this book I attribute to my LORD JESUS and the strength HE has provided me; and if you will note, my first book, CHOSEN VESSEL was written rather sporadically, and with unnecessary references to the sins of self pleasure and alcohol drinking. The point is, this book you are reading right now was written by the LORD JESUS through me; I know you can tell the difference between the writing styles. This book flows better, whereas my first book was written primarily while experiencing my affliction of schizophrenia. The disease I have has not subsided; I just wanted you reading this to know that my LORD JESUS helped me write my first book, and is writing this book through me, schizophrenia included.

Chapter 3

Consider this: the WORD says in NEHEMIAH 8:10 that the joy of the LORD is our strength. What joy *does* our LORD JESUS have now that HE is glorified and sitting at the right hand of our GOD? From my finite mind, and limited understanding, I would begin by saying that HE has the joy of knowing HE accomplished *the* most important act of sacrifice to the entire human race; HE has the joy and satisfaction of knowing HE had and has the authority to take and keep the keys of Hell and death from Satan; HE knows that one day very soon, HE will be united with HIS BRIDE, the Church, and actually, being Eternal, HE *is* there with us even now, for HE is everywhere and every when; Omnipotent, and Omnipresent. LORD JESUS knows that HE is KING over *all* creation, with the power and authority to carry it out; HE is back HOME, in the presence of HIS (and our) Holy Heavenly FATHER. HIS joy is *full*. As will ours be when we are HOME. Until then, we must see HIS joy as the source of our strength. We must continue to pray and watch for HIM, loving HIM as HE is: our KING.

There is also our privilege of praying according to the will of GOD, ensuring we are praying what is best for every situation we pray for; but remember, FATHER GOD can answer our prayers any one of three ways: Yes, No, and Yes, but wait upon ME for it. Even the LORD JESUS was denied HIS request at the Garden of Gethsemane, for FATHER GOD knew the only path for HIS SON. I believe the best prayer is what LORD JESUS prayed:

> "Not MY will, but THY will be done." Now that we have the precious HOLY SPIRIT, we can pray in the SPIRIT; ensuring that we are praying according to the will of GOD.

The WORD says:

Likewise the SPIRIT also helpeth our infirmities: for we know not what we should pray for as we ought: but the SPIRIT itself maketh intersession for us with groanings which cannot be uttered. And HE that searcheth the hearts knoweth what *is* the mind of the SPIRIT, because HE maketh intersession for the Saints according to *the will* of GOD.

(ROMANS 8:26,27)

When reading the WORD of GOD, we must take it seriously, seeing in between the lines with the blessed insight that our LORD JESUS gives us when we seek HIS understanding of HIS WORD. I personally like the King James Version, because at one time the LORD GOD spoke to me and said this: "Take the coat from off thy shoulders, and pray." HE actually said this to me when I was preparing to leave without praying to HIM. The use of the word "thy" stuck with me, and since then, all communication with me has used this type of language; that of the King James Version. I believe some of the effectiveness of the WORD of GOD is lost in some of the other more lenient versions of the Bible. The following is an example. Even in the New King James Version, the exhortation is changed to not include the request of FATHER GOD that peace be present with those who are in CHRIST JESUS.

In the King James Version, Paul the apostle ended his letters with exhortations of this kind:

Peace *be* with you all that are in CHRIST JESUS.

(1st Peter5:14)

The italicized word "be" denotes peace as being present. Paul was speaking peace on all those who are in JESUS CHRIST. Just as he spoke the grace of our LORD JESUS on us:

The grace of our LORD JESUS CHRIST *be* with you. Amen.

(1st THESSALONIANS 5:28)

Receive it! We all need peace in this turbulent world. And grace is something every believer knows they need in abundance; grace and peace that are presently with us because Paul spoke it upon us in his letters; letters that were written by the HOLY SPIRIT through him, for our benefit.

I am indebted for life to FATHER GOD's HOLY SPIRIT; HE speaks to me throughout the day, and warns me of incoming temptation; HE reminds me of FATHER GOD's promises, and leads me in seeing them manifested in my life. For as the WORD says:

> "Howbeit when HE, the SPIRIT of Truth, is come, HE will guide you into all truth: for HE shall not speak of HIMSELF; but whatsoever HE shall hear, *that* shall HE speak: and HE will show you things to come. HE shall glorify ME: for HE shall receive of MINE, and shall show *it* unto you.

> (JOHN 16: 13,14)

HE *knows me* completely; and knows just the right words to speak to cheer me up, or to motivate me; HE *is* my counselor in all matters spiritual, and even the day to day matters. I have never met a more sensitive companion than the HOLY SPIRIT. I love HIM.

Chapter 4

How does LORD JESUS affect my daily life? Right now, my LORD JESUS, through HIS HOLY SPIRIT, is guiding my fingers on the keyboard for what to write. My mornings start off with prayer in HIS Name. Actually, it *is* my LORD JESUS Who is leading those prayers through my dead vessel. I was given this revelation *as* I was praying one day. The LORD JESUS showed me that since I *am* dead, and my life is hid with HIM, in FATHER GOD, and since THEY are inside this vessel, it is now my LORD JESUS Who is leading the prayers through me:
The WORD says:

> Set your affection on things above, not on things on the earth. For ye are dead, and your life is hid with CHRIST in GOD.

> (COLOSSIANS 3:2,3.)

And the one that tells me it is LORD JESUS within me:

> I am crucified with CHRIST: nevertheless I live; yet not I, but CHRIST liveth in me...

> (GALATIANS 2:20.)

Throughout the day, HE counsels me on any number of situations, again through HIS HOLY SPIRIT; the precious HOLY SPIRIT. Again I must confess my sin of grieving the HOLY SPIRIT by my inaction at times, when HE would lead something to be done for a fellow brother or sister. All, I know hurt, or grieved HIM. There is nothing in my life that hurts worse than thinking I have hurt my best Friend.

The presence of my LORD in my life gives me peace. The WORD says:

> "Peace I leave with you, MY peace I give unto you: not as the world gives, give I unto you. Let not your heart be troubled, neither let it be afraid."

(JOHN 14:27)

LORD JESUS *is* the Prince of Peace. Naturally HIS presence gives peace. And HE *is* inside the bodies we are in, with us, in our hearts. Again I want to reiterate- Let not your heart be troubled, neither let it be afraid. HE is with us till the end, which is really the beginning, for after this life is over, Eternity with HIM begins! When a million years have passed, I've heard it said Eternity is just beginning. Actually, there is no time before the Throne in Eternity. Eternity is Life without regard to time (for those of us who are in Heaven); think about Eternity in the Lake of Fire: never ending anguish and torment for those who have forsaken the WORD. It says:

> But the fearful, and unbelieving, and the abominable, and murderers, and whoremongers, and sorcerers, and idolaters, and all liars, shall have their part in the lake which burneth with fire and brimstone: which is the second death.

(REVELATION 21:8.)

Where the last verse mentions "abominable," I was shown the WORD where it talks about the 6 things that the LORD hates, 7 which are an abomination to HIM:

> A proud look, a lying tongue, and hands that shed innocent blood, a heart that deviseth wicked imaginations, feet that be swift in running to mischief, a false witness that speaketh lies, and he that soweth discord among brethren.

(PROVERBS 6: 16-19)

Each of us has been tempted with any number of these things; to the degree that each of us is still temptable. Paul said that he was the least of the Saints, but I know I am. I have done some of the most hypocritical, abominable things in the sight of my GOD; yet HE, in HIS amazing Mercy, led me to repentance each and every time, forgiving me of my sins, and washing me clean again with my LORD JESUS' blood. It will be the true test of my faith, when this book comes out, and those who know what kind of man I have been, see what kind of man I have been changed into by my FATHER GOD's Grace. I want them to know that I am sorry for all that I have done in their sight, and hope that they will see true repentance in my words here. And that they too, will know the peace that I have come to know and walk in now, by accepting LORD JESUS into their hearts.

Webster's Collegiate Dictionary defines "abomination" as "extreme disgust, or hatred." I mean HE really loathes these 7 things. Why does the LORD hate these 7 things? Let's take a look at this. First is a proud look. It was FATHER GOD Who designed Lucifer to be HIS greatest creation, one who would be the epitome of praise to the FATHER. When iniquity was found in him (EZEKIEL 28:13-19), Lucifer was cast out of Heaven, with 1/3rd of all the angels, who chose to follow him. (REVELATION 12:4). I say all this to get to this point: pride goes before destruction and a haughty spirit before a fall. (PROVERBS 16:18)

I believe the LORD hates a proud look because, per HIS WORD, HE knows what pride does to each of us. A proud look involves pride in oneself, or one's accomplishments, and we know that self (the old man) must die, and the new man put on, the one created after FATHER GOD (EPHESIANS 4: 22-24).

Pride sent HIS creation Lucifer to eternal damnation in the Lake of Fire, along with all the demons that were angels. LORD JESUS rules over all creation-Heaven and Hell, *and* the Lake of Fire. HE reigns forever. It is my focus to be there in Heaven with HIM, for all Eternity.

Pride in us gets in the way of relationships, especially with the FATHER, and our LORD JESUS; even FATHER GOD told us about the importance of humility when HE told us in 2nd CHRONICLES 7:14, "If my people, which are called by my Name, shall humble themselves, and pray, and seek my face, and turn from their wicked ways; then will I hear from Heaven, and forgive their sin, and will heal their land."

It just was given me to think about something; a proud look also says that I alone can do this; I don't need GOD. Now there are things that don't require FATHER GOD's intervention, but it's the circumstances that *do*, that when you look with a proud look and say within yourselves that you can do it without GOD, that it miffs the LORD.

We know before destruction the heart of a man is haughty, and before honor *is* humility. (PROVERBS 18:12). Humility is the opposite of pride. Pride leads to destruction; along with the fear of the LORD, humility leads to life, riches, and honor. (PROVERBS 22:4).

A proud look involves arrogance, which Webster's Collegiate Dictionary defines "arrogant" as "exaggerating one's own worth, or importance often in an overbearing manner." To put it simply, we are a created being, created by the Supreme Being. We need to learn to keep our place and not see ourselves as more than we are-dust and water, and soul, and spirit, given by FATHER GOD, in our LORD JESUS CHRIST. But important enough to have the LORD die for us; our worth is in CHRIST JESUS.

One such example of my own arrogance was trip to my Mom's house. I was on the highway, cruising above the speed limit. The LORD spoke to me to slow down (rather sternly) and I got angry with HIM, and shouted "no, I will not slow down!" Wouldn't you know, the very next car to pass me was a State Trooper, who pulled me over and gave me a ticket for over $100.00! After the incident was over, pride again flared up in me, since my feelings were hurt, but that soon gave way to a new found humility, and eagerness to hear the voice of my LORD when HE speaks.

The next thing that the LORD hates is a lying tongue. This one to me seems rather obvious. Satan is a liar, and the father of them (John 8:44). Anyone who wants to lie, and loves to lie, will spend Eternity in the Lake of Fire (REVELATION 21:8) if one wants to be like their old master, they will share in his punishment. Now I have lied "little white lies," and sometimes I get in too deep in a conversation, and one of the obvious ways out of it is to give a little white lie- "I have to go now, I've got something on the stove." I mean we don't want to hurt the other person's feelings, by saying the truth: "I have to go now; your cornball humor is getting on my nerves." A lie is a lie, regardless of whose feelings you are trying to protect. Think about how you could handle a situation like this.

The LORD knows that a lying tongue, HE has judged worthy of the Lake of Fire. True repentance, after confessing the sin(s) of lying, and being forgiven by the LORD JESUS, will right the wrong, and prevent you from a one way ticket down.

The next thing that the LORD hates, are hands that shed innocent blood. We're talking now about civilian casualties, and abortion. I believe that life starts upon conception; any aborting of that life is an abomination to the LORD. "Thou shalt not kill." It doesn't get any plainer than that.

A tale comes to mind, about a cat that was left at my house, which stayed outside. My friend, (who left the cat with me), and I decided to go to the local mall, and proceeded to get into the car to leave. When I backed out, I ran over the cat, and broke its back. It was flailing, and in very much agony. I jumped out of the car and grabbed the cat, bent on a mercy killing. I grabbed the cat by the neck and squeezed till the neck was broken. It was one of the hardest things I have ever had to do in my life, but this, I believe was not shedding innocent blood. It was a mercy kill. I say this to clear my own conscience.

The next thing that the LORD loathes is a heart that deviseth wicked imaginations. This one I am well versed in. We have been taught from an early age that imagination is a good thing, but not in the LORD's eyes. It can also be said that imagination in the mind is different than imaginations of the heart. The heart is very complex thing. It is one thing to let a child use the mind to imagine flying like a butterfly, and like me, to imagine in my heart, having adulterous relations with my neighbor's wife. Let's take this in a new direction. What are the various things one might imagine in their heart? I mean, besides having adulterous sex. Pride in one's heart in one's self is a double whammy. This is a wicked imagination, as well.

"As a man thinketh in his heart, so is he."

(PROVERBS 23:7).

Let's break it down; two words- wicked, and imagination. First of all, not all imaginations are wicked. Those of the mind I believe can be all right. But I also believe that *any* imaginations of the heart are wicked, and come from pride. Take my imaginations about adultery with my neighbor's wife; the pride is that I feel I could be with her, (in my heart, I imagine this). That is evil, and wicked.

Wicked imaginations take you away from reality, which take you away from the reality of FATHER GOD, and the LORD JESUS. Anything that takes us away from them is a bad thing, and I can see why the LORD hates that; HE wants us as close to HIMSELF as we can possibly be, for our own protection against Satan's attacks, and to be ready for the LORD's imminent return.

Feet that be swift in running into mischief…think about a parent, with their child. Very few things make a parent madder than a child who is acting up. And for the FATHER, our acting up and getting into sin makes HIM very angry. First of all, sin separates us from our FATHER; and again what do parents feel like when they are separated from their children? If it is something that they have done to themselves, it angers us, doesn't it? The first thing we want to do is get our children back, which is exactly what FATHER GOD does, by HIS goodness, leading us back in repentance, to be forgiven by HIM.

The next thing that is an abomination to the LORD is a false witness, which speaks lies. There are a couple of things that pop into my mind when I think of "false" anything's. False gods, who lead people astray, like money and power, and the "false Christ's," that are spoken about in MATTHEW 24:24. As far as a false witness, it is obvious to me why the LORD hates this. I believe HE hates it because of the result to the person being witnessed to. I believe that some people are given one chance to see the Kingdom of GOD, and the person that delivers that message has one shot at seeing that person into the Kingdom. It is only FATHER GOD's Grace that gives more time, and other opportunities.

Have I ever been a false witness? The answer is sadly, yes. I believe that actions speak as loudly as words; and people don't forget what you do. They may forgive, but rarely forget. The hardest place to be a witness is at home. That's where people really see what you are made of.

My witness that spoke lies was back in my early days of being a Christian, when I was still afraid of showing my true colors (my Christian colors). A thought just hit me; it's different if you are intentionally false witnessing, and speaking lies; what I was doing was covering up the truth; the truth that I am a Child of GOD, and a Brother to my LORD JESUS CHRIST.

A false witness is someone who intentionally lies to someone else about the truth of LORD JESUS, not only of HIMSELF, but in their lives as well. I have done this sporadically (much to my dismay, and FATHER GOD, and my LORD JESUS as well),

through my actions, and probably more importantly, my inaction in people's lives that are involved with me. I have tried to keep my words to a minimum, knowing that each idle word will be given account thereof on the Day of Judgment. I wouldn't say that I have spoken lies, just have false witnessed through my actions and inactions. I have not spoken when it was appropriate to do so, in LORD JESUS' defense, which I believe is the same as lying. So I have asked for forgiveness for these sins, and have received it.

He that sows discord among the brethren would be a part of the flock, the brethren being the Body of CHRIST. To sow discord, would be to plant seeds of gossip and lies, pitting each other against one another; or as the WORD says in EPHESIANS 4:3, "Endeavoring to keep the unity of the SPIRIT in the bond of peace." Rather this, which was just spoken, is what we need to be doing. Sowing discord goes directly against the WORD of GOD, which thing the LORD hates.

Chapter 5

The WORD is my guideline for what to do, (and what *not* to do). The WORD truly is the instruction manual for our lives. When was the last time you read the WORD? In my book, which I praise HIM for! Now put down my book, and pick up the complete work of the LORD, and READ IT! Pray for HIS understanding, and pray that the seed of the WORD goes into good ground in your heart, unstolen by Satan. Fight and win in the Name of JESUS the temptation to ignore the HOLY SPIRIT's leading to read. You will be pleasantly surprised and delighted how FATHER GOD speaks to you from HIS WORD.

You will also be amazed at how Satan will try to dissuade you from reading, or at the very least to get your attention off of what you are reading. Have you ever tried to read and found that you didn't get anything out of what you were reading because your mind was filled with all kinds of thoughts you thought were your own? It was Satan, doing what he does best, stealing, killing, and destroying. That's why I urge you to pray that the seed of the WORD remain unstolen in your heart. Pray also for the understanding of the WORD, for this is what allows Satan to steal- when we don't understand what we have read. Again, the WORD says:

> The thief cometh not, but for to steal, and to kill, and to destroy: I am come that they might have life, and that they might have *it* more abundantly.

> (JOHN 10:10)

"When anyone heareth the word of the Kingdom, and understandeth *it* not, then cometh the wicked *one*, and catcheth away that which was sown in his heart. This is he which received seed by the wayside."

(MATTHEW 13:19.)

The sanctified life, which is the one that is rid of the old nature, or at least has it in its place: DEAD, will enjoy more of the abundant life LORD JESUS spoke of. Those lives that walk in abundant life aren't cluttered up with everyday cares, which LORD JESUS warns us of in MATTHEW 13:7:

> "He also that received seed among the thorns is he that heareth the WORD; and the cares of this world, and the deceitfulness of riches, choke the WORD, and he becometh unfruitful.

Be careful that you don't get too caught up in worldly things. I know to a certain degree we have to be involved in the world we live in, but don't let it choke out the WORD of GOD in your lives.

My LORD JESUS has a problem with the music I listen to right at this very moment in the writing of this book you are reading now. In my I-tunes library on my computer I have classical, Christian, contemporary today music, and some of the older classic rock tunes I used to listen to before I became a Child of GOD. I just started listening to them again when I got this computer I'm writing this book with. My LORD is dealing with me at this very moment about some of the music I listen to. I can't write Christian writings while listening to some of the music I have in my library, so I put on in the back ground some good Christian music, and it uplifts my spirit while I am writing. Let me tell you what the LORD spoke to me 2 nights ago. I was listening to an artist which I knew was questionable in FATHER GOD's ears. I went on the information website, and got the words to the song I was listening to. I realized with the HOLY SPIRIT's leading that this music was Satan spawned, and I spoke the words out loud "this is devil music!" And at that moment the LORD spoke to me and said, "What is this music doing on MY computer?" I immediately repented of having it on HIS computer (which I think is neat, considering I believe that being dead to self, I have no possessions), and took it off. I'm sure that some of the other music I have in my library will end up in the recycle bin too. Praise GOD! Life is a series of learning experiences, and with my LORD's help, I will learn my lessons well.

I just pray that I don't cause anyone who believes in LORD JESUS to sin because of the music I still listen to. After all the WORD says:

> "But whoso shall offend one of these little one which believe in ME, it were better for him that a millstone were hanged about his neck, and *that* he were drowned in the depth of the sea. Woe unto the world because of offences! For it must needs be that offences come; but woe to that man by whom the offence cometh!"

> (MATTHEW 18:6,7.)

Knowing that my LORD JESUS loves me enough to correct me (constantly) and that HE is patiently working me to the point of sanctification and death of self, I have an acute sense of HIS presence in my life.

Chapter 6

HIS presence within me gives me confidence. Again the WORD:

> Seeing then that we have a great high priest, that has passed into the heavens, JESUS the SON of GOD, let us hold fast *our* profession. For we have not an high priest which cannot be touched with the feeling of our infirmities; but was in all points tempted like as *we are, yet* without sin. Let us therefore come boldly unto the Throne of grace, that we may obtain mercy, and find grace to help in time of need.

> (HEBREWS 4:14-16)

> Cast not away therefore thy confidence, which hath great recompense of reward.

> (HEBREWS 10:35.)

Imagine the confidence the LORD JESUS had when HE was waiting for the angry mob to come and take HIM away. HE knew HE had more than legions of angels at HIS command; yet HE knew that HE had to let HIMSELF be taken away for our sake. Except for the presence of HIS love for us, it must have been frustrating for HIM knowing this. At any point of HIS torture and crucifixion HE could have called upon GOD to send those angels and release HIM. But HE didn't. HE finished the cup that FATHER GOD had for HIM to drink, and paved the super highway of access to the FATHER by HIS death, and resurrection; demolishing the partition between us. Oh, love HIM! LORD JESUS! YOU have done <u>everything</u> for us! Nothing is impossible to us now, because of what YOU have accomplished. I praise YOU, praise YOU, Praise YOU, PRAISE YOU!

The very thought of my LORD being alive, after being dead, and the truth that HE is alive forevermore, and that I will by HIS grace and mercy spend eternity with HIM causes my heart to shout, and a heavy sigh to pass my lips, knowing I must wait patiently for HIS return or my death, whichever comes first.

The WORD says:

> According to my earnest expectation and *my* hope, that in nothing I shall be ashamed, but *that* with all boldness, as always, so now also CHRIST shall be magnified in my body, whether *it be* by life or by death. For to me to live *is* CHRIST, and to die *is* gain.
>
> (PHILIPPIANS 1:20,21)

The problem in waiting patiently for LORD JESUS, is my tendency to be distracted from what I am supposed to be doing. And I have no excuse, for I am quite sure what I am supposed to be doing. When I get distracted, the HOLY SPIRIT redirects me back to writing these books, and living for my LORD each and every day; watching for my LORD's return, and praying for the Body of CHRIST. Praying for the changes I need, to become into my LORD JESUS' image. One of the most important is the manifestation of the fruit of the HOLY SPIRIT in our lives.

Chapter 7

The fruit of the SPIRIT is love, joy, peace, patience, kindness, gentleness, goodness, faithfulness, longsuffering, and self control: against such things there is no law.

(GALATIANS 5:22,23)

The path to sanctification for the born again Christian involves the perfecting of this fruit in our lives, and the removal of all the fruit of the flesh, including the carnal mind. This must happen, for as the WORD says:

Be not deceived; GOD is not mocked: for whatsoever a man sows, that shall he also reap. For he that soweth to his flesh shall of the flesh reap corruption; but he that soweth to the SPIRIT shall of the SPIRIT reap life everlasting.

(GALATIANS 6:7,8)

I would like to tell you of the changes in me that the HOLY SPIRIT has been doing, regarding HIS fruit in my life. I could write a whole book just on the fruit of the SPIRIT. Let's begin with LOVE. The WORD says that GOD *is* love; and to love HIM is to obey HIM. The HOLY SPIRIT has taught me this, along with the heart knowledge that I *am* loved by the FATHER, SON, and HOLY SPIRIT; also that I love me, as THEY love me; at least, I am learning to; as well as learning to love my fellow man, looking beyond the physical to the soul and spirit of each individual. This all ties together quite wonderfully-the loving of ourselves (as FATHER,

SON, and HOLY SPIRIT love us), and loving our neighbor as ourselves; the loving of GOD with all our hearts, souls, minds, and strength which are the 2 greatest commandments. Having love manifested in my life, all around me, I feel THEIR arms around me even as I write this. I really do love THEM! And you can't help loving your neighbor when you love FATHER GOD and LORD JESUS. This is even scriptural, for the WORD says:

> We love HIM, because HE first loved us. If any man says, I love GOD, and hateth his brother, he is a liar: for he that loveth not his brother whom he has seen, how can he love GOD whom he hath not seen? And this commandment we have from HIM, that he who loveth GOD loves his brother also.

> (1st JOHN 4:19-21.)

> By this we know that we love the Children of GOD, when we love GOD, and keep HIS commandments.

> (1st JOHN 5:2.)

Next of the fruit of the SPIRIT is JOY. Joy is especially dear to me, for I suffer from schizophrenia and have long bouts with battling depression. But I can tell you that you can have joy in the midst of depression, even though this sounds contradictory. The joy of the SPIRIT is knowing we are saved from the wrath to come, through the Blood of LORD JESUS CHRIST which covers us; It is a joy that is higher than the happiness we tend to walk in from this world. Joy comes from above, and rests on all those who believe in LORD JESUS. The only thing I've seen be manifested as far as joy is concerned is continually walking in the knowledge of my own salvation, and the hope of my LORD's imminent return for me. There again, love plays its part in joy as well. As the LORD JESUS said:

> "As the FATHER hath loved ME, so have I loved you: continue ye in MY love. If you keep MY commandments, ye shall abide in MY love; even as I've kept MY FATHER's commandments, and abide in HIS love. These things have

I spoken unto you, that MY joy might remain in you, and *that* your joy might be full."

(JOHN 15:9-11)

The fruit of PEACE, *even* the very peace of GOD, which passes all understanding, has been a long time in coming for me. The demons of schizophrenia have, for the longest time succeeded in stealing my peace, by telling me lies, saying that I wasn't saved because of my continual sinning. FATHER GOD's forgiveness would bring back HIS peace only for Satan to steal it again. This went on for many years, until I finally got a hold of the knowledge of the truth that the Prince of Peace, my LORD JESUS, is inside my heart, and that HIS very presence there brings peace. Not of this world, but peace that you just kind of heave a big, grateful sigh and accept in your heart and mind.

...But to be spiritually minded is life and peace.

(ROMANS 8:6.)

The revelation of being spiritually minded came to me some years back; I would speak in the HOLY SPIRIT, HE would speak back to me in HIS language, then the interpretation would come to my mind. There was peace in knowing I had from the best source, the only true source, the perfect answer, comment, understanding of every situation I applied this to. I still have a *long* way to go to have *perfect* peace; the one described in PSALMS 37:37:

Mark the perfect *man*, and behold the upright: for the end of *that* man *is* peace.

I may not achieve this kind of peace in this world; but I am on the road that leads to it. Until then, I am content with the peace that passes all understanding, keeping my heart and mind through CHRIST JESUS my LORD.

Chapter 8

PATIENCE. Most people are scared to even mention it in prayer, afraid that FATHER GOD will do something terrible to them, like make them wait for something they have asked for. "GOD grant me patience, and I want it NOW!" Well, the way that it works is like this: First, FATHER GOD shows you that you have a need of patience; like HE did me by showing me HEBREWS 10:36 in RHEMA (the WORD alive). Next, LORD JESUS prays of the FATHER through your dead vessel for patience for you. (You still think it's you that is praying, don't you); then comes every kind of patience producing situation you could ever imagine, that FATHER GOD puts you through. HIS Mercy and Grace are present, and HE will not give you more than you can take, though you can take far more than you are willing to admit to, because you don't want to have to go through any more than you have to in receiving the patience LORD JESUS asked for you; right?

Actually, it's not that bad. It's kind of humorous, if you look at it in the right way. You know that you (LORD JESUS through you, actually) have asked for patience; You then *know* it's coming-the patience producing situations. You can tell just what FATHER GOD is *trying* to teach you by what comes your way. Patience with your fellow Christians, or patience with yourself (that's a big one), or even patience with GOD HIMSELF; waiting upon the LORD GOD for answers to prayers that HE tells you , you have to wait upon HIM for. All of these I have been through, to some degree; and I admit, it wasn't fun going through them at the time, but now, I wouldn't trade going through those lessons for anything. I found PROVERBS to be an excellent source of guidance in understanding myself as I went through these lessons.
The WORD says:

He that is slow to anger *is* better than the mighty; and he
that ruleth his spirit than he that taketh a city.

(PROVERBS 16:32.)

I used to get violently angry with myself over minor things prior to
learning patience. Now, it's like the anger is taken away, and replaced with
a peaceful knowledge that.

I *can* do all things through CHRIST JESUS which
strengtheneth me.

(PHILIPPIANS 4:13.)

I find it neat that all of the fruit of the SPIRIT are intertwined and
rely on each other to make they themselves work; as in the Body of
CHRIST, each part is reliant on the others to make the whole body work
in unison.
As the WORD says:

But speaking the truth in love, may grow up into HIM in
all things, which is the head *even* CHRIST: from whom
the whole body fitly joined together and compacted by
that which every joint supplieth, according to the effectual
working in the measure of every part, maketh increase of
the body unto the edifying of itself in love.

(EPHESIANS 4:15,16.)

If you desire to grow in the SPIRIT, ask for the patience to complete
FATHER GOD's Holy perfect will and in that patience *to* accomplish it.
HE will; and you may cringe when the situations come at you; be prepared
for doubt to come at you, for some of the situations may seem like you have
done something wrong, when it is only FATHER GOD working in your
life. Let me explain what a doubt producing situation might look like. In
my own life, when something like my son's car breaking down taxes my
patience, not to mention my wallet, I might feel like GOD was angry at
me; when in truth, all of the details to getting my son's car fixed produced

patience and experience. And faith, for I had to believe in faith for my finances to stay on budget to fix his car.

Believe me, you won't regret going through those lessons when they are accomplished. There is such a feeling of confidence in me now, knowing that I can handle any circumstance with patience and understanding; knowing also that HE Who is inside me won't let anything get too much for me to handle. LORD JESUS has pressed my boundaries, making what I can take that much more. I find peace in the patience I have gained by my LORD JESUS' Grace and Mercy. It's one of those things I knew I needed, but didn't want to go through what it takes to get it. FATHER GOD knew this, and knew also just how to get me to want what HE knew I needed. I am so glad that HE has our best in mind when LORD JESUS prays these things for us. The WORD describes generally what brings patience:

> And not only *so*, but we glory in tribulations also: knowing that tribulation worketh patience; and patience, experience; and experience, hope: and hope maketh not ashamed; because the love of GOD is shed abroad in our hearts by the HOLY GHOST which is given to us.

> (ROMANS 5:3-5.)

The confidence I have now *is* from the experience I gained from the working of my patience. That is like exercising faith; only it is patience that is being exercised. Praise GOD, for patience producing situations!

This same concept is true for anything you ask for; If it's love you need for the poor, for example, FATHER GOD lets you know you lack love for them; LORD JESUS intercedes for you before the FATHER, asking for that love using your own voice, so you are edified at the same time; then comes the encounters with the poor, where you will be placed in a position to either turn away in disgust, or begin to love them. All the while, FATHER GOD is molding you on the inside, leading your heart to open up towards them. We are works in progress, this you may or may not know. FATHER GOD is constantly working in us, and through us for other's benefit.

The WORD says:

Being confident of this very thing, that HE which hath begun a good work in you will perform *it* until the day of JESUS CHRIST.

(PHILIPPIANS 1:6.)

Be patient therefore, brethren, unto the coming of the LORD. Behold, the husbandman waiteth for the precious fruit of the earth, and hath long patience for it, until he receive the early and latter rain. Be ye also patient; stablish your hearts: for the coming of the LORD draweth nigh.

(JAMES 5:7,8.)

Another fruit of the SPIRIT is KINDNESS. To be kind and compassionate, like LORD JESUS was to the crowds of people who followed HIM where ever HE went, healing their sick and diseased, is what I feel we should be doing; for as LORD JESUS said:

"Go ye into all the world, and preach the Gospel to every creature. He that believeth and is baptized shall be saved; but he that believeth not shall be damned. And these signs shall follow them that believe; in MY Name shall they cast out devils; they shall speak with new tongues; they shall take up serpents; and if they drink any deadly thing, it shall not hurt them; they shall lay hands on the sick, and they shall recover."

(MARK 16:15-18.)

Now let me make this very clear. LORD JESUS' Words are not telling you to drink anything poisonous just to prove it won't hurt you. For the WORD says in MATTHEW
4:5-7 when the Devil tried to get LORD JESUS to jump off the temple knowing the angels would bear HIM up in their arms:

"It is written again, Thou shalt not tempt the LORD thy GOD.

What it *is* saying is that we need to be witnessing, both with our lifestyles, and to the lost; and they who believe and are baptized will be saved. And that we should be doing these things even now-laying hands on the sick and seeing them recover. For as the LORD JESUS said:

> "Verily, verily, I say unto you. He that believeth on ME,
> the works that I do shall he do also; and greater *works* than
> these shall he do; because I go unto MY FATHER."

> (JOHN 14:12.)

My LORD JESUS has been deepening me in the fruit of kindness, with mercy, and compassion, to the point of seeing my children's friends being witnessed to through my lifestyle, with words of encouragement and love for them. They pretty much stayed at my apartment throughout the summer preceding their going off to college this year. My LORD has taught me so much this summer, and done some magnificent things in me as far as the fruit of the SPIRIT. This is what I meant by *my* tribulation- having upwards of 10 kids here at my place at one time staying the night, the weekend, the week! This went on for three and a half months. And I love each and every one of them (my kids, especially). I consider each one of them a part of my flock.

Kindness is the trait that causes us to look upon each other with compassion, helping one another through the trials and tribulations we must all endure in this life. The kindness I saw in my LORD JESUS' eyes when HE showed me HIS magnificent Face in mine (see CHOSEN VESSEL, chapter 3) gives me confidence that HE has my best in mind at all times; and not only me, but all who love HIM, who share in the Body of my LORD JESUS, the Church.

The 6th fruit listed in the WORD of GOD is GOODNESS. Because there are so many connotations for the word "good," I must go to the WORD once again:

> And, behold, one came and said to HIM, Good Master,
> what good thing shall I do, that I may have eternal life?
> And HE said unto him, why callest thou ME good? *There*
> *is* none good but One that *is*, GOD: but if thou wilt enter
> life, keep the commandments."

> (MATTHEW 19:16,17)

We know that FATHER GOD is good; we also know that LORD JESUS is the SON of GOD, and in Heaven with GOD, as GOD, with the HOLY SPIRIT the three as ONE. Therefore, to me, LORD JESUS is good. We know that the goodness of GOD leads us to repentance; (ROMANS 2:4) I can only say that the quality of goodness we, as Christians have is because of Who is in our hearts; and THEY convey that quality through our dead vessels. Have you ever been in the presence of someone so SPIRIT filled that you just wanted to tell them everything? I have. And I believe it is because of the presence of FATHER GOD within them leading me to repentance, and the desire of confessing our faults one to another that we might be healed (JAMES 5:16):

> Confess *your* faults one to another, and pray one for another, that ye may be healed. The effectual fervent prayer of a righteous man availeth much.

The 7th of the fruit listed is GENTLENESS. I've always been gentle, but the workings of the HOLY SPIRIT in my life have resulted in my being as the WORD says in 2nd PETER:

> Flee also youthful lusts: but follow righteousness, faith, love, peace, with them that call upon the LORD out of pure heart. But foolish and unlearned questions avoid, knowing they do gender strifes. And the servant of the LORD must not strive; but be gentle unto all *men*, apt to teach, patient, in meekness instructing those that oppose themselves; if GOD peradventure will give them repentance to the acknowledging of the truth; and that they may recover themselves out of the snare of the Devil, who are taken captive by him at his will.

(2nd PETER 2: 22-26.)

FAITHFULNESS accounts for the 8th of the fruit of the HOLY SPIRIT. This I have utterly failed in, so I will speak of FATHER GOD's faithfulness to me. HE has, and always will be the most faithful Friend; HE and my LORD JESUS, and THEIR HOLY SPIRIT; when I would walk away willingly (which I don't even know *why* I do), except a <u>bad</u> case of pure disobedience, THEY would wait patiently while

FATHER GOD's goodness led me back to repentance. I have learned much from *THEIR* faithfulness, all of which I pray right now in my LORD JESUS' Name to put into practice.

> And the very GOD of peace sanctify you wholly; and I *pray GOD* your whole spirit and soul and body be preserved blameless unto the coming of our LORD JESUS CHRIST. Faithful *is* HE that calleth you, who also will do *it*.

(1ˢᵗ THESSALONIANS 5: 23,24.)

Chapter 9

I was just shown something I had not even considered. Our Holy Heavenly FATHER, our LORD JESUS, *and* the HOLY SPIRIT are *perfect*. As for having all of the fruit of the HOLY SPIRIT working in them, they are perfectly enabled in every way. We, as the Body of CHRIST need to be praying for the fruit of the HOLY SPIRIT to be manifested in our lives (as I am led to each and every morning). If I were not as treacherous and hard headed, and thick skulled, I would be a lot farther along in this manifestation. But by HIS Grace, and Mercy I am learning.

I just realized something. The King James Version is not what I have been following in these descriptions of the fruit of the SPIRIT. It has been from the New King James Version, which has 9 fruits; whereas the King James Version has 9 also, but describes them differently. In the King James Version, Meekness and temperance are defined in Webster's Dictionary as taking insult patiently, and without resentment; and moderation in action, thought or feeling; respectfully. That last one is a little hard to understand and apply. I do understand why the writers of the New King James Version adapted it to say kindness and self-control. This is what I meant by the different versions having different meanings. In this case, I prefer the New King James Version.

LONGSUFFERING is next in my descriptions of the fruit being manifested in our lives. As with the others, longsuffering is needed to ensure patient understanding between ourselves. It is a quality that allows us to maintain enduring relationships without bitterness or resentment; to put it simply, we put up with each other. I love longsuffering; FATHER GOD has been such with me for all of my life, and especially since I became HIS Child. Without it, I fear HE would have given up on me a long time ago. That's why I love it.

SELF-CONTROL is a quality we *all* need desperately. I think this is the one that the King James Version called temperance. Moderation; self-control I feel nails it more on the head. Since self must die, the act of controlling self would mean to me at the time between being born of the SPIRIT, and when self actually dies. We all deal with "self" on a daily basis. Our reactions when we walk in the flesh, are from our "selves." Satan tempts us through our "self." To control self would mean to me not allowing self to rule, but letting our spirit rule our lives. I remember when I was still lost, self ruined my life by causing me to try and commit suicide. Living in the SPIRIT, letting my spirit be one with the HOLY SPIRIT, communing with HIM minute by minute, is the only way to live this life.

Chapter 10

Such is the fruit of the HOLY SPIRIT; wonderful and the only way to maintain a healthy relationship with FATHER GOD and our LORD JESUS. Seeing them manifested in our lives by constant, consistent prayer; realizing the hard truth, that there is no middle ground; no fence sitting. We are either glorifying FATHER GOD in the bodies we are in, or we are walking in the flesh. The WORD can't get any more explicit:

> For they that are after the flesh do mind the things of the flesh; but they that are after the SPIRIT the things of the SPIRIT. For to be carnally minded *is* death; but to be spiritually minded is life and peace. Because the carnal mind *is* enmity against GOD: for it not subject to the law of GOD, neither indeed can be. So then they that are in the flesh cannot please GOD.

> (ROMANS 8:5-8)

Webster's Collegiate Dictionary defines enmity as hatred or ill will. I don't know about you, but I definitely don't want anything of mine to hate GOD. I therefore choose *not* to walk in the carnal mind. It takes a conscience daily decision to do this; to be spiritually minded is to dwell upon things that the HOLY SPIRIT brings to your mind and thoughts; Taking care to watch for Satan bringing things in his guise of an angel of light. The WORD of GOD says:

> And no marvel; for Satan himself is transformed into an angel of light. Therefore it is no great thing if his ministers

also be transformed as the ministers of righteousness; whose end shall be according to their works.

(2nd CORINTHIANS 11:14,15.)

Being schizophrenic, I have dealt with deception most of my adult life; voices that sound like the real thing would tempt and torment me with almost truths that would lead to doubt in myself and worst of all, doubt in my own salvation in my LORD JESUS. All the while it was being taken advantage of by Satan, who would then speak in the guise of this "angel of light;" telling me half truths, using the WORD to bring doubt in my heart, just as he did to LORD JESUS in the wilderness. I've often wondered why FATHER GOD would tell me I wasn't saved. Now I know who it was-Satan. Schizo voices I can deal with; but some of the things I am told are very hard to tell whether they are true or not. When I was led to this verse in my Owner's Manual (my Bible), it pretty much dismayed me, because I thought, "How am I going to tell what's true or real now?" Then my LORD JESUS counseled me to check what they were telling me against the WORD. This was back in the eighties, and it still is my guide line in advising me, if I am not sure.

Chapter 11

Complacency is defined by Webster's Dictionary as "Self satisfaction especially when accompanied by unawareness of actual dangers or deficiencies." Complacency is why we run yellow lights; complacency in our spiritual lives threatens every aspect of our walk with FATHER GOD. Putting our 'self-ish' wants ahead of the Kingdom of GOD, oblivious to the dangers of being carnally (worldly) minded, I am led to the WORD once again:

> This I say therefore, and testify in the LORD, that you henceforth walk not as other Gentiles walk, in the vanity of their mind, having the understanding darkened, being alienated from the life of GOD through the ignorance that is in them, because of the blindness of their heart: who being past feeling have given themselves over unto lasciviousness, to work all uncleanness with greediness.

> (EPHESIANS 4:17-19)

Let me first say that this verse has described me, and I didn't even know it till the LORD allowed me to temporarily live the life of GOD; and it was fantastic! HE led <u>everything</u>, and talked to me as HE did; HIS timing was (and is) perfect in everything HE did for, and through me, for other's benefits. It was not until FATHER GOD allowed me to realize where I lacked, that I started to pray for the life of GOD to be permanent in my life. In order for this to happen, the WORD has to be manifested in me. Namely, being renewed in the spirit of my mind (EPHESIANS 4:23) through constant reading and digesting of the WORD of GOD, always praying that the seed of the WORD go into good ground in my heart, and remain there unstolen by Satan.

Now I have been distracted by Satan, through worldly cares, (money matters, children's college etc.), and don't always follow my own advice, but I do know that the process for sanctification involves constant exposure and ingestion of the WORD of GOD.

About the verse just mentioned, (EPHESIANS 4:17-19), Webster's Dictionary defines lasciviousness as 'lewd, or lustful'. I had just skipped over this verse in reading it, thinking it didn't pertain to me. But do you realize how easy it is to walk in the vanity of your mind? Read a newspaper; watch a television program; listen to the radio. Your mind goes active, and before you know it, you are leaning on your own understanding, which is directly against the WORD of GOD (PROVERBS 3:5).

Be careful here. Once the reading of the WORD has given you something to think about, don't let JAMES 1:23.24 happen to you. The verse goes thusly:

> For if any man be a hearer of the WORD, and not a doer, he is like unto a man beholding his natural face in a glass: for he beholdeth himself, and goeth his way, and straightway forgetteth what manner of man he was.

Pray for FATHER GOD's understanding, and let the WORD change you into LORD JESUS' image!

I want to explain just what happened to me when my LORD JESUS showed me my understanding being darkened from dwelling in the vanity of my mind. (EPHESIANS 4:17,18) FATHER GOD, in HIS infinite mercy allows me to function even in the midst of a darkened understanding. Actually, HE provides the capability to function on all but the most extreme levels of understanding we walk in; the exception being the act of suicide. But I am talking about the Body of CHRIST, who I believe are protected on all sides from the onslaught of Satan's desire to kill us; I believe he is content with disarming us, making us unusable to LORD JESUS through hypocrisy and pride, and the dwelling in the vanity of our minds. When I say 'protected on all sides' I don't mean that FATHER GOD can't take us Home whenever HE chooses, like in tornados and floods, and in forest fires; or like my dear, sweet mother, who is dying of idiopathic pulmonary fibrosis (the hardening of her lungs). When she is taken Home, she and her LORD JESUS will have something in common—they will have both died of suffocation. And they both will live forever.

Unguarded thoughts, dwelling in the wicked imaginations that Satan put in my mind; all this darkened my understanding. I don't know why, except it's the way FATHER GOD designed us. LORD JESUS allowed me to realize the difference between my dimmed understanding and when I was allowed to live the life of GOD for those few days. Now, thank GOD, I have been led in the direction that will have me living the life of GOD again, this time permanently. (This is what I am praying and believing for). When I say that I lived the Life of GOD, I don't mean that I haven't been living *for* GOD; it merely means that I was living the excellencies of the *abundant* life that is in LORD JESUS which most people miss out on because they *do* dwell in the vanity of their mind most of the time.

Chapter 12

Seasoned men and women of GOD need to take new lambs under their wings, or rather should I say that our LORD JESUS takes them under HIS Wings through our dead vessels; entrusting their feeding to us per the WORD:

> Feed the flock of GOD which is among you, taking the oversight *thereof,* not by constraint, but willingly; not for filthy lucre, (money) but of a ready mind; neither as being lords over *GOD's* heritage, but being examples to the flock. And when the Chief Shepherd shall appear, you shall receive a crown of glory that fadeth not away.
>
> (1st PETER 5:2-4)

My point is this: each of us has a flock. Whether it is our families, or business associates, or just each person who FATHER GOD brings along our path on a daily basis; we need to take care of them in prayer, especially the young in CHRIST, and stay aware of MATTHEW 25:31-46: which says:

> "When the SON of man shall come in HIS Glory, and all the Holy angels with HIM, then shall HE sit upon the Throne of HIS Glory: And before HIM shall be gathered all nations: and HE shall separate them one from another, as a shepherd divideth *his* sheep from the goats: And HE shall set the sheep on HIS right hand, but the goats on HIS left. Then shall the KING say unto them on HIS right hand, Come, ye blessed of MY FATHER, inherit

the Kingdom prepared for you from the foundation of the world: For I was an hungered and you gave ME meat: I was thirsty and you gave ME drink: I was a stranger and you took ME in: Naked, and you clothed ME: I was sick , and you visited ME: I was in prison, and you came unto ME: Then shall the righteous answer HIM, saying, LORD, when saw we THEE an hungered, and fed *THEE*? Or thirsty, and gave *THEE* drink? When saw we THEE a stranger, and took *THEE* in? Or naked, and clothed *THEE*? Or when saw we THEE sick, or in prison, and came unto *THEE*? And the KING shall answer and say unto them, Verily I say unto you, inasmuch as you have done *it* unto one of the least of these MY brethren, you have done it unto ME.

Then shall HE say also unto them on the left hand, Depart from ME, ye cursed, into everlasting fire, prepared for the Devil and his angels: for I was an hungered, and you gave ME no meat; I was thirsty, and you gave ME no drink: I was a stranger, and you took ME not in: naked, and you clothed ME not: sick, and in prison, and you visited ME not. Then shall they also answer HIM, saying , LORD, when saw we THEE an hungered, or athirst, or a stranger, or naked, or sick, or in prison, and did not minister unto THEE? Then shall HE answer them, saying, Verily I say unto you, inasmuch as you have done *it* not to one of the least of these, you did *it* not unto ME. And these shall go away into everlasting punishment: but the righteous into life eternal."

There again, we need to take the WORD at face value; if we indeed looked at every circumstance as if we were dealing with LORD JESUS, it would change drastically what we did, and for the better. I will endeavor to do this, and I ask for YOUR Grace upon me as I do, my LORD JESUS, in THY Name, I ask it. And praise YOU for it!

It can add a lot of pressure and stress constantly thinking that every person you encounter, you are dealing with the LORD JESUS; perhaps the best way to see these situations is The Golden Rule: Do unto others as you would have them do unto you; or as the WORD says:

"And as ye would that men should do to you, do ye to them likewise."

(LUKE 6:31.)

Stop when you see the woman with the hood of her car open, and the look of desperation on her face; take the time sometime to visit an old folk's home and just visit with someone who has no one. If this doesn't sound like something you would be comfortable doing, yet you want to do what LORD JESUS wants you to do, PRAY for compassion, and love for others in action. You'll be surprised and delighted when FATHER GOD starts sending people your way. Ask for HIS Mercy as HE does these things, to take it slow and easy on you. HE will; FATHER GOD knows what you can take, and more importantly what you need. We all need to get out of ourselves and start looking to the needs of others, and to love them as FATHER GOD and LORD JESUS do.

Chapter 13

Consider this: Could you accept the true virgin conception and birth of the LORD JESUS CHRIST with your own intellect? Does it not take faith to even begin to accept it? I am citing the difference between the way a man's intellect sees, and that which must be seen through the eyes of faith. Now remember what faith is.

The WORD of GOD says:

> Now faith is the substance of things hoped for and the evidence of things not seen.

> (HEBREWS 11:1)

After applying this verse to the virgin birth of LORD JESUS, it makes sense to me, (In faith). It cannot be believed through my own understanding. The tangible evidence is missing, but the evidence to be believed in faith is very present. I begin to understand why the WORD says:

> Trust in the LORD with all your heart, and lean not on your own understanding; acknowledge HIM in all your ways, and HE will direct your paths.

> (PROVERBS 3:5,6)

The raising of LORD JESUS from the dead is similar, except there were witnesses to LORD JESUS being alive after HE was crucified, died and was buried. It is we who must now in faith, believe that HE *was* raised from the dead.

Chapter 14

My next subject is accountability. Most people realize that they will be accountable for what they've done in their lives when they die. As the WORD says:

> For we must all appear before the judgment seat of CHRIST that each one may receive the things *done* in *his* body according to that he has done whether it *be* good or bad.

(2nd CORINTHIANS 5:10)

But there is accountability in this life as well. Most of the things that happen to us, whether good or bad are because of FATHER GOD's righteous judgments. Rewards come to those that do good, for as the WORD says:

> Blessed *is* the man that walketh not in the counsel of the ungodly, nor standeth in the way of sinners, nor sitteth in the seat of the scornful.

(PSALM 1:1)

FATHER GOD *blesses* us when we listen to HIS counsel; HE *blesses* us when we stand with the Righteous, and stay away from those who scorn HIS ways. HIS blessings *are* the reward. On the other hand, HIS righteous judgment on the wicked is spoken of many times in PROVERBS:

The curse of the LORD is in the house of the wicked: but
HE blesseth the habitation of the just.

(PROVERBS 3:33.)

A naughty person, a wicked man, walketh with a froward
mouth. He winketh with his eyes, he speaketh with his
feet, he teacheth with his fingers; frowardness *is* in his
heart, he deviseth mischief continually: he soweth discord.
Therefore shall his calamity come suddenly; suddenly shall
he be broken without remedy.

(PROVERBS 6:12-15.)

Webster's Dictionary defines froward as 'Habitually disposed to
disobedience and opposition.' FATHER GOD's righteous judgment is
the calamity that will come on this person if they continue to disobey.
What I want to relay is the fact that daily events include FATHER GOD's
intervention; not that we go through this life doing what we want, and *then*
we stand before LORD JESUS receiving what we get for what we did and
didn't do. GOD is actively participating in our lives, aware completely of
our thoughts, and our hearts, and reacts to them and what we do in, and
with them either by blessing us for good, or reproving us for bad with HIS
righteous judgments. Remember, FATHER GOD *is* love. HIS reproof is
done in love.
The WORD says:

MY son, despise not the chastening of the LORD; neither
be weary of HIS correction: for whom the LORD loveth,
HE correcteth; even as a father the son *in whom* he
delighteth.

(PROVERBS3:11,12.)

The wicked (those who don't have and won't have LORD JESUS in
their heart) are another matter in the LORD's eyes.
The WORD says again:

The LORD *is* far from the wicked: but HE heareth the prayer of the righteous.

(PROVERBS 15:29.)

There is no respect of persons with FATHER GOD, for as the WORD says:

"You have heard that it hath been said, Thou shalt love thy neighbor, and hate thine enemy. But I say unto you, love your ememies, bless them that curse you, do good to them that hate you, and pray for them which despitefully use you, and persecute you; that you may be the Children of your FATHER which is in Heaven: for HE maketh HIS sun to rise upon the evil and the good, and sendeth rain on the just and the unjust."

(MATTHEW 5:43-45.)

Chapter 15

A truly important part of sanctification is obedience to the WORD, and to FATHER GOD's Commandments; for as the WORD says:

> "Therefore whosoever heareth these sayings of MINE, and doeth them, I will liken him unto a wise man, which built his house upon a rock: and the rain descended, and the floods came, and the winds blew, and beat upon that house; and it fell not: for it was founded upon a rock. And everyone that heareth these sayings of MINE, and doeth them not, shall be likened unto a foolish man, which built his house upon the sand: and the rain descended, and the floods came, and the winds blew, and beat upon that house; and it fell: and great was the fall of it."

(MATTHEW 7:24-27.)

Obedience in my own life has been a long time coming; I still in stressful times willfully disobey my HOLY Heavenly FATHER, much to my dismay (and HIS too, I believe) I have worn out my welcome several times, and have played the part of the prodigal son as well. If it weren't for FATHER GOD's magnificent Mercy (which HE is rich in), and the Grace of my HOLY LORD JESUS, my Advocate, for as the WORD says again:

> My little children, these things I write unto you that you may not sin. And if anyone sins, we have an Advocate with the FATHER, JESUS CHRIST the Righteous.

(1ˢᵗ JOHN 2:1.)

I am quite sure I would have been banned from the Kingdom a long time ago. I know that my LORD JESUS has plead my case before the FATHER more times than I am comfortable telling you; and in truth, I *was* banned from the Kingdom once (as you read in CHOSEN VESSEL, chapter 5), and FATHER GOD had exceeding abundant Mercy upon me and allowed me to ask LORD JESUS back into my heart. I have learned the hard way to obey my HOLY FATHER and my LORD JESUS; and yes, I am familiar with HEBREWS 10:26,27:

> For if we sin willfully after that we have received the knowledge of the truth, there remaineth no more sacrifice for sins, but a certain fearful looking for of judgment and fiery indignation, which shall devour the adversaries.

I don't know what to tell you about that. All I know is that I *know* FATHER GOD and my LORD JESUS love me. And by their Mercy and Grace I *am* still saved. I have repented of the evil works that I once was captive to; and daily have to beg forgiveness for desiring those things when Satan tempts me with them again. It's an ongoing process of being strengthened against temptation, being knowledgeable of the WORD:

> Resist the Devil and he will flee from you.
>
> (JAMES 4:7.)

> Neither give place to the Devil.
>
> (EPHESIANS 4:27.)

> Above all, taking the shield of faith, wherewith ye shall be able to quench all the fiery darts of the wicked.
>
> (EPHESIANS 6:16.)

> Let us hear the conclusion of the whole matter: Fear GOD and keep HIS Commandments: for this *is* the whole *duty*

of man. For GOD shall bring every work into judgment, with every secret thing, whether *it be* good, or whether *it be* evil.

(ECCLESIASTES 12:13,14.)

If we're going to talk obedience to the commandments, let us write them down here. My heart tells me that some of you reading this will skip over this part; but *please* read them carefully.

And GOD spake all these words, saying, I *am* the LORD thy GOD, which have brought thee out the land of Egypt, out of the house of bondage.

(EXODUS 20:1,2)

Now I am going to break in at various pertinent places with comment by the leading of the HOLY SPIRIT, so let us begin with these words of GOD; each of us has an Egypt that we were or are bound in bondage to; whether it be secular television, or alcohol, or cigarettes, for example. The list of things that one could be bound in is long, but the good news is FATHER GOD has, and is leading us out of these bondages. LORD JESUS broke the back of bondage in our lives. We only need to ask for HIM to deliver us out these things, and HE will. It will require your patience, so be prepared.
Back to the WORD:

Thou shalt have no other gods before ME.

(EXODUS 20:3)

What is considered a "god" in 21st century thinking? Something that one would worship comes to mind. Something one would trust in comes to mind also. Money is undoubtedly one of the big ones in today's economy. Another big one is "self." The worship of our selves above GOD sounds rather narcissistic, yet it is fully reasonable to me, for it is what Lucifer was charged with prior to his being forced out of Heaven.
The WORD says:

Thou hast been in Eden the garden of GOD; every precious stone *was* thy covering, the sardius, topaz, and the diamond, the beryl, the onyx, and the jasper, the sapphire , the emerald, and the carbuncle, and gold: the workmanship of thy tabrets and of thy pipes was prepared in thee in the day that thou wast created. Thou *art* the anointed cherub thatcovereth; and I have set thee *so*: thou wast on the holy mountain of GOD; thou hast walkedup and down in the midst of the stones of fire. Thou *wast* perfect in thy ways from the day thou wast created, till iniquity was found in thee.

(EZEKIEL 28:13-15.)

And HE said unto them, "I beheld Satan as lightning fall from Heaven."

(LUKE 10:18.)

How art thou fallen from Heaven, O Lucifer, son of the morning! *How* art thou cutdown to the ground, which didst weaken the nations! For thou hast said in thine heart, I will ascend into Heaven, I will exalt my throne above the stars of GOD: I will sit also upon the mount of the congregation, in the sides of the north: I will ascend above the heights of the clouds: I will be like the most High. Yet thou shall be brought down to hell, to the sides of the pit

(ISAIAH 14:12-15.)

Lucifer, because of pride, made his self image like that of GOD HIMSELF. To be worship-ped, which we know FATHER GOD and LORD JESUS are only to be worshipped.
Satan still longs to be worshipped, as evidenced by his request of LORD JESUS in the wilderness:

Again, the Devil taketh HIM up into an exceeding high mountain, and showingHIM all the kingdoms of the world, and the glory of them; and saith unto HIM, all these things will I give thee, if THOU wilt fall down and worship me.

(MATTHEW 4:8,9.)

We know what LORD JESUS said to Satan:

"Get thee hence, Satan: for it is written, Thou shalt worship the LORD thy GOD, and HIM only shalt thou serve."

(MATTHEW 4:10)

Thinking too highly of oneself leads to pride; and we know what the WORD says about pride:

Pride *goeth* before destruction, and an haughty spirit before a fall.

(PROVERBS 16:18)

Chapter 16

Let's go on to the meat of the matter; the 12 commandments:

> Thou shalt not make unto thee any graven image, or any likeness *of anything* that *is* in heaven above, or that *is* in the earth beneath, or that *is* in the water under the earth:

(EXODUS 20:4.)

Let me stop for a moment to give you Webster's definition of "graven image." It is 'an object of worship usually carved of wood or stone: idol.' OK, now on to the WORD:

> Thou shalt not bow down to them, nor serve them: for I the LORD thy GOD *am* a jealous GOD, visiting the iniquity of the fathers upon the children unto the third and fourth *generation* of them that hate ME; and showing mercy upon thousands of them that love ME, and keep MY commandments.

(EXODUS 20: 5,6.)

At first, I was worried that the graven image thing meant that I had to get rid of all my pictures of people, and animals and such; and the figurines I bought at the zoo of animals. It's all in how you view it; if I worshipped these things, then they would be "graven images," and would therefore need to be gotten rid of; along with my attitude of worshipping them. But what about the posters of prominent people that are available to be purchased? Some of these kids, (and adults, too) almost worship these people. I feel in my spirit that it's like the WORD says in MATTHEW:

> "Then if any man shall say unto you, Lo, here *is* CHRIST, or there; believe *it* not. For there shall arise false Christ's, and false prophets, and shall show great signs and *wonders*; insomuch that, if *it were* possible, they shall deceive the very elect."

(MATTHEW 24:23,24.)

I'm not saying that these people *are* false Christs; it's just that they seem to set themselves up as that which should be worshipped; which I feel is dead wrong. I am waiting to see these people who really *are* the false Christs that our LORD JESUS spoke of. The time we are in history is scary indeed, except for the hope that our LORD's return is indeed nigh at the door. Oh, blessed hope that we who believe have!

Let's return to the WORD:

> Thou shalt not take the Name of the LORD thy GOD in vain; for the LORD will not hold him guiltless that taketh HIS Name in vain.

(EXODUS 20:7.)

Now when I get very frustrated, I have a tendency to curse and I have at times taken my FATHER's Name in vain. I have begged for forgiveness, and PRAISE HIM, have received it. Now in line with what I have been saying here, I know I need to ask for patience in frustrating situations; but the reason I haven't, *is* because of my tendencies, and I don't want to incur the wrath of my FATHER while I am learning that lesson. HE will have to present it in a merciful way for it to be asked of HIM. On to the WORD again:

> Remember the Sabbath day, to keep it holy. Six days shalt thou labor, and do all thy work: but the seventh day *is* the Sabbath of the LORD thy GOD: *in it* thou shalt not do any work, thou, nor thy son, nor thy daughter, thy manservant, nor thy cattle, nor thy stranger that *is* within thy gates: for

in six days the LORD made heaven and earth, the sea, and all that in them *is,* and rested the seventh day: wherefore the LORD blessed the Sabbath day, and hallowed it.

(EXODUS 20: 8-11.)

LORD JESUS spoke about this in MATTHEW; rather HE spoke about doing good on the Sabbath:

And HE said unto them, "What man shall there be among you, that shall have one sheep and if it fall in to a pit on the Sabbath day, will he not lay hold on it and lift it out? How much then is a man better than a sheep? Wherefore it is lawful to do well on the Sabbath days."

(MATTHEW 12:11,12.)

LORD JESUS spoke additionally adding that which hadn't been revealed yet of HIS FATHER's WORD for our benefit; about killing; about adultery, and forswearing yourself. And I believe that HE means it when HE says keep the Sabbath day holy.

What is the 21st century equivalent of this mean? Lost revenues and time and a half lost! Yet, it's the WORD of GOD. I know of people who can't get a job, because they won't work Sundays. I admire that, though the strictness of it does seem to be a little too much in this time and place. Remember what was said about complacency? We must get back to strict obedience to the WORD.

Honor thy father and thy mother: that thy days may be long upon the land which the LORD thy GOD giveth thee.

(EXODUS 20: 12)

The problem with obeying this commandment goes back quite a ways; into the relationships that dad and mom had with their parents, and siblings. Some children don't even know *who* their father or mother *is*; this commandment is meaningless to them. But in the same way as the Sabbath, it still needs to be done. With constant prayerful contact with FATHER

GOD in LORD JESUS' Name, the very thought of honoring parents (known or unknown) becomes like a daily devotional thing; where you are aware of your parents, and if you still live with them, whether it be preteen, or taking care of them when they are older, honoring them means to honor that which you have, first of all; obedience to their authority, as LORD JESUS did when HE was 12. The WORD says in LUKE, chapter 2, the young JESUS stayed behind in Jerusalem while HIS mother and Joseph, unaware that HE had done so, kept traveling. Three days later they found HIM in the temple. When they confronted HIM, HE said, "How is it that ye sought ME? Know ye not that I must be about MY FATHER's business?" HE then went back with them to Nazareth and was subject unto them for the next 18 years, learning the trade of carpenter. I believe this was JESUS' way of honoring Joseph, and HIS mother, being obedient to them.

This brings up an awkward point; what about abusive parents, or neglectful parents, who don't deserve the respect of their children? It's hard to honor someone who is never there for you, or who beats you; I feel the Day of Judgment will bring the necessary light to an almost impossible scenario. So what about our responsibility now? Do what you can, with what you have. Regular parents, step parents, foster parents, and single parents- all need to be honored.
Verse 13 of EXODUS 20:

> Thou shalt not kill. LORD JESUS adds in MATTHEW 5:21:

> "Ye have heard that it was said by them of old time, Thou shalt not kill; and whosoever shall kill shall be in danger of the judgment: but I say unto you, that whosoever is angry with his brother without a cause shall be in danger of the judgment: and whosoever shall say to his brother Raca, (that is to say, worthless) shall be in danger of the council: but whosoever shall say, Thou fool, shall be in danger of hell fire."

Much more sensitive, don't you think? Forgive and forget, as FATHER GOD does. This means that when that person pulls out in front of you, scaring the heck out of you, damaging your pride, (not to mention your sense of security), you must do the obvious thing- immediately forgive that person, praying for them, so they don't do that again. It's all about staying in contact with FATHER GOD. If you had prayed for GOD's Holy perfect timing in your life for that day, you might not have been where that person would have pulled out in front of you. Then again, FATHER GOD is always working in us; you may have been in that scenario *to* bring about the lesson of forgiveness. Don't count GOD out of your life! HE is present with us! Talk to HIM like HE is. LORD JESUS is present with us, as is HIS HOLY SPIRIT. Communicate with them!

EXODUS chapter 20, verse 14 says:

Thou shalt not commit adultery.

LORD JESUS added in MATTHEW 5:27, saying,

"Ye have heard that it was said by them of old time, thou shalt not commit adultery: But I say unto you, that whosoever looketh on a woman to lust after her hath committed adultery with her already in his heart."

This works both ways, you know.

Thou shalt not steal.

(EXODUS 20:15)

I am inclined to believe that just thinking about doing something wrong is sinning in our thoughts; for as the WORD says:

For the weapons of our warfare *are* not carnal, but mighty through GOD to the pulling down of strongholds; casting down imaginations, and every high thing that exalteth itself against the knowledge of GOD, and bringing into captivity every thought to the obedience of CHRIST.

(2nd CORINTHIANS 10:4,5.)

Thou shalt not bear false witness against thy neighbor.

(EXODUS 20:16)

Consider this: What *is* your witness? Isn't it your lifestyle, the way you live, both in secret and out in the open for everyone to see? Anything that is not witnessing *for* the LORD JESUS is false witnessing, and needs to be confessed and forgiven by HIM. I have had to do this several times in my private life, and I am glad for it-thankful to my LORD JESUS and HOLY Heavenly FATHER that they care about my spiritual condition.

> Thou shalt not covet thy neighbor's house; thou shalt not covet thy neighbor's wife, or his manservant, or his maidservant, or his ox, or his donkey, or anything that *is* thy neighbor's.

> (EXODUS 20:17)

So the 10 commandments go; but the 2 most important ones are yet to be displayed here:

> "Thou shalt love the LORD thy GOD with all thy heart, all thy soul, and thy entire mind. This is the first and great commandment. And the second is like unto it, Thou shalt love thy neighbor as thyself. On these two commandments hang all the law and the prophets."

> (MATTHEW 22: 37-40.)

It's not so difficult to love someone with all your being; just consider what HE has done for you; EVERYTHING. My GOD is absolutely present in my life; HE directs my steps, delights in my way, and thankfully picks me up when I fall. Learning obedience to these commandments is not a grievous thing. It just takes love for FATHER GOD, HIS SPIRIT, and our LORD JESUS, and walking in the faith HE has given us.

The process of learning obedience, whether it be to the HOLY SPIRIT when HE leads, or just obeying the commandments of FATHER GOD on a daily basis; being a doer of the WORK, and not a forgetful hearer, is a big part of sanctification. Again the WORD:

> Who in the days of HIS flesh, when HE had offered up prayers and supplications with strong crying and tears unto HIM Who was able to save HIM from death, and

was heard in that HE feared; though HE were a SON, yet HE learned obedience by the things which HE suffered; and being made perfect, HE became the author of eternal salvation unto all them who obey HIM…

(HEBREWS 5:7-9.)

LORD JESUS, the process by which we are changed into THINE image is an absolute necessary one, because how YOU find us at THY return is where we will spend eternity. That is why YOU tell us to watch and pray, for we know not at what hour YOU are coming. YOUR Words:

"Let not your heart be troubled, ye believe in GOD, believe also in ME. In MY FATHER's house are many mansions: if *it were* not so, I would have told you. I go to prepare a place for you. And if I go and prepare a place for you, I will come again, and receive you unto MYSELF; that where I am, *there* ye may be also."

(JOHN 14:1-3)

Again, YOUR Words:

"Watch therefore: for ye know not what hour your LORD doth come. But know this, that if the goodman of the house had known in what watch the thief would come, he would have watched, and would not have suffered his house to be broken up. Therefore be ye also ready: for in such an hour that ye think not the SON of man cometh. Who then is a faithful and wise servant, whom his LORD hath made ruler over HIS household, to give them meat in due season? Blessed *is* that servant, whom his LORD when HE cometh shall find so doing. Verily I say unto you, that HE shall make him ruler over all HIS goods." "But and if that evil servant shall say in his heart, my LORD delayeth HIS coming; and shall begin to smite *his* fellow servants, and to eat and drink with the drunken; the LORD of that servant shall come in a day when he looketh not for *HIM,* and in an hour he is not aware of, and shall cut him asunder, and appoint *him* his portion with the hypocrites: there shall be weeping and gnashing of teeth."

(MATTHEW 24:42-51.)

Consider this: *billions* of people and each will be maneuvered to either be found ready or to be caught unawares. Each of us interacting at the time; the absolute *power* to accomplish this that our LORD JESUS commands… YOU *are truly awesome*, my LORD JESUS!

Being found ready *is* my goal. The prayers that my LORD JESUS prays through me of the FATHER for my benefit, and those we pray for, are geared for preparing us for HIS return, or our death, whichever comes first. Many are called, few are chosen. I have been chosen to write to you in hopes of seeing you all sanctified by the WORD. The WORD says:

And HE gave some, apostles; and some, prophets; and some, evangelists; and some, pastors and teachers; for the perfecting of the saints, for the work of the ministry, for the edifying of the Body of CHRIST: till we all come in the unity of the faith, and of the knowledge of the SON of GOD, unto a perfect man, unto the measure of the stature of the fullness of CHRIST…

(EPHESIANS 4: 11-13.)

Again the WORD:

Husbands, love your wives, even as CHRIST also loved the Church, and gave HIMSELF for it; that HE might sanctify and cleanse it with the washing of water by the WORD, that HE might present it to HIMSELF a glorious Church, not having spot, or wrinkle, or any such thing; but that it should be holy and without blemish.

(EPHESIANS 5:25-27)

Chapter 17

Those, to whom it is given to the task of perfecting the saints, even if it is through the written word, must be, and walk worthy of the LORD JESUS CHRIST. I have been given directly the task of writing to you, and I am the first to admit, I am not worthy. I don't think that anyone is *really* worthy, it is a matter of getting up after you have fallen, letting LORD JESUS wash you in HIS Blood and getting back to the doing of FATHER GOD's will. Now I have done evil things while being a Christian that I will not speak of again, for they are forgiven, both now and forever. Every now and then I still feel the condemnation from Satan even though FATHER GOD just told me that I am completely forgiven. I go on because I am led to by HIS HOLY SPIRIT. I strive to remain repentant, and continue to listen for the HOLY SPIRIT's voice, and leading.

I have found that the HOLY SPIRIT will not allow me to write as HE directs with anything that is not of HIM present; I'd like to say now that being repentant and turning away from evil things is all I ask to want. I'd like to thank YOU, my LORD JESUS, right now for YOUR understanding and mercy in ridding me of any appearance of evil.

As YOU showed me a couple of nights ago, while I was resting on my bed, looking up at the ceiling, my eyes open, I beheld a vision of Hands, reaching out on to my computer keyboard, resting there. I was shown that these Hands were YOUR Hands, LORD JESUS, and that YOU'RE is the ONE who guides my writings. I have been blessed with the knowledge of what I need to be doing, and I am doing it; all in the Grace and Mercy of YOU, my HOLY LORD JESUS and THEE, my HOLY Heavenly FATHER.

What is then our responsibility in the path FATHER GOD has chosen us on? Truly to keep believing in the LORD JESUS in faith; and as 1st THESSALONIANS 5:14-24 admonishes:

> Now we exhort you brethren, warn them that are unruly, comfort the feebleminded, support the weak, be patient toward all *men*. See that none render evil for evil unto any *man*; but ever follow that which is good, both among yourselves, and to all *men*. Rejoice evermore. Pray without ceasing. In everything give thanks: for this is the will of GOD in CHRIST JESUS concerning you. Quench not the SPIRIT. Despise not prophesyings. Prove all things; hold fast that which is good. Abstain from all appearance of evil. And the very GOD of peace sanctify you wholly; and *I pray GOD* your whole spirit, and soul, and body be preserved blameless unto the coming of our LORD JESUS CHRIST. Faithful *is* HE that calleth you, who also will do *it*.

It is a good idea to listen to your heart when deciding on what to do; it's an even better idea to listen *with* your heart when hearing FATHER GOD as HE teaches us, either through HIS WORD, or through circumstances that are designed to bring about righteousness and holiness in our lives. Sanctification achieved by reacting to circumstantial stimuli, or circumstances like, the break-up of a relationship; or finding out that FATHER GOD really does love us by realizing HIS forgiveness to a particularly stubborn sin; or going through a painful good-bye to a loved one with a terminal illness; all these things are very effective in bringing about patience, learning forgiveness, learning to love despite not receiving love in return, in essence, perfecting the fruit of the HOLY SPIRIT. I am led to believe that the WORD of GOD is the key to sanctification.

Webster's Dictionary defines 'sanctify' as: To free from sin: to purify. LORD JESUS said HIMSELF, in JOHN 17:17, as HE was praying to FATHER GOD:

> "Sanctify them through THY truth: THY WORD is truth. As THOU hast sent ME into the world, even so I have sent them into the world. And for their sakes I

sanctify MYSELF, that they also might be sanctified through the truth."

The LORD JESUS *is* the WORD of GOD:

In the beginning was the WORD, and the WORD was with GOD, and the WORD was GOD. The same was in the beginning with GOD. All things were made by HIM; and without HIM was not anything made that was made. In HIM was life; and the life was the light of men.

(JOHN 1:1-4.)

I love talking about my LORD JESUS. HE is Eternal, there before anything was, and as HE said in JOHN 8:58:

JESUS said unto them, "Before Abraham was, I AM."

That just *thrills* me! I break out into HOLY SPIRIT laughter every time I hear that.

There are more descriptions of LORD JESUS *being* before anything was:

The LORD possessed me in the beginning of HIS way, before HIS works of old. I was set up from everlasting, from the beginning, or ever the earth was. When *there were* no depths, I was brought forth; when *there were* no fountains abounding with water. Before the mountains were settled, before the hills was I brought forth: while as yet HE had not made the earth, or the fields, or the highest part of the dust of the world. When HE prepared the heavens, I *was* there: when HE set a compass upon the face of the depth: when HE established the clouds above: when HE strengthened the fountains of the deep: when HE gave to the sea HIS decree, that the waters should not pass HIS commandment: when HE appointed the foundations of the earth: Then I was by HIM, *as* one brought up *with HIM:* and I was daily *HIS* delight, rejoicing always before HIM; Rejoicing in the habitable

part of HIS earth; and MY delights were with the sons
of men.

(PROVERBS 8:22-31.)

I once had a vision of FATHER GOD sitting upon HIS Throne, contemplating every last detail of creation, from the beginning of GENESIS, through Eternity with us all in Heaven; every detail of the thoughts of man, our reactions, and interactions with each other. Every placement of every rain drop was purposed by HIM. Consider this: did you ever have a reaction to a rain drop falling down your neck? GOD planned that, as humorous as HE probably found that, your reaction was of more interest to HIM. Thanking HIM for the rain; thanking HIM for each and every placement of the rain drops; laughing with HIM as you wiggle around trying to dry the drop that HE just dripped down your back. FATHER GOD *has* a sense of humor! You just have to look and listen for it.

Delight thyself also in the LORD, and HE will give thee
the desires of thine heart.

(PSALMS 37:4)

The LORD JESUS delights in you, so delight yourself in HIM! Take HIM at HIS word. *HE loves you.* If you haven't received the LORD JESUS into your heart, and are not yet born again, *now is the time.* All it takes is a verbal prayer, (or a silent prayer if you prefer), confessing from your heart that you are a sinner, that you have sinned against GOD, and that you want to be completely forgiven of your sins and washed in the blood that LORD JESUS shed when HE died on the cross for you; Believe in your heart that LORD JESUS died and rose again on the third day after his death. Then ask HIM into your heart. HE will come into your heart, with the HOLY FATHER, and HIS HOLY SPIRIT, and if you have done this, Praise GOD! You are now Heaven bound! Nothing in Heaven or earth can take THEM away from you. As the WORD says:

Who shall separate us from the love of CHRIST? Shall tribulation, or distress, or persecution, or famine, or nakedness, or peril, or sword? As it is written, for THY sake we are killed all the daylong; we are accounted as

65

sheep for the slaughter. Nay, in these things we are more than conquerors through HIM that loved us. For I am persuaded, that neither death, nor life, nor angels, nor principalities, nor powers, nor things present, nor things to come, nor height, nor depth, nor any other creature, shall be able to separate us from the love of GOD which is in CHRIST JESUS our LORD.

(ROMANS 8:35-39.)

Chapter 18

Consider this: From the beginning, men and women were created to be partners; GENESIS 2:18-25 says:

> And the LORD GOD said, "*It is* not good that man should be alone; I will make him a helper that is comparable to him. And out of the ground the LORD GOD formed every beast of the field and every fowl of the air; and brought *them* unto Adam to see what he would call them: and whatsoever Adam called every living creature, that *was* the name thereof. And Adam gave names to all cattle, and to the fowl of the air, and to every beast of the field; but for Adam there was not found an help meet for him. And the LORD GOD caused a deep sleep to fall upon Adam, and he slept: and HE took one of his ribs, and closed up the flesh instead thereof; and the rib, which the LORD GOD had taken from man, made HE a woman, and brought her unto the man. And Adam said, this *is* now bone of my bones, and flesh of my flesh: she shall be called Woman, because she was taken out of Man. Therefore shall a man leave his father and mother, and shall cleave unto his wife: and they shall be one flesh. And they were both naked, the man and his wife, and were not ashamed.

(GENESIS 2:18-25.)

What I'd like you to consider is this: believe it or not, I believe we were meant to live like that. I know it's difficult to entertain the thought of millions of naked people populating the earth, oblivious to each other's nakedness; but that's because of the carnal mind we possess now from the knowledge of good and evil we obtained after eating the forbidden fruit in the Garden of Eden.

What's interesting and distressing to me, now that FATHER GOD and my LORD JESUS have blessed my understanding, is that the true blood line started with Adam and Eve has been disrupted by fornication and incestuous sex; causing, to put it simply, that the people who were originally meant to be together by the *perfect* will of FATHER GOD, ended up pairing with partners that they weren't meant to be with. FATHER GOD in HIS mercy had planned as part of HIS perfect will that less than perfect partners were to *be* perfect for each other; for as you see in society there *are* those who are truly perfect for each other. I have heard it said that FATHER GOD has a perfect plan for each and every one of us. I believe this to be true. Those who don't see FATHER GOD's perfect will done in their lives are missing all the opportunities for LORD JESUS and FATHER GOD to bless and save those through them, who would have been blessed and saved if they had been doing FATHER GOD's perfect will. It is truly disheartening to think about all the people who are missing the Kingdom of GOD because we are not where we should be in HIM. That's why I am writing about the process of sanctification, and stressing the importance of it.

Read the WORD! Pray in the HOLY SPIRIT! Pray before you read the WORD that is remain in your heart in good ground, unstolen by Satan. Don't let Satan have a foot in your door the way I have in the past. I know all about this. I know his devices and the way in which he works, and deceives and lies to us. Don't let him do it! Don't let him show anything on the screen of your mind, or tell you anything in the guise of self- Iam this, or we should be doing this or that. Anything that makes you think it was you saying it. Force him into a full frontal attack, where he must speak to you himself. Then you can tell him where to go in LORD JESUS' precious Name! Just as LORD JESUS did, when HE was tempted in the wilderness. "Get thee hence, Satan, for it is written…" Use the sword of the SPIRIT, the WORD of GOD in an offensive attack back at him. Force him to back down in LORD JESUS' Name. He must obey what you command in LORD JESUS' Name. Don't be afraid of him. LORD JESUS has defeated him at Calvary. Walk in victory with LORD JESUS in your heart, with all thoughts in submission to HIM.

Remember, if you simply ignore him (Satan) he will not go away; unless he chooses to go away. If you find Satan tempting you, or trying to plant seeds of unrighteousness in your mind or heart, you <u>must</u> command him in LORD JESUS' Name to leave. I do this and it works! The idler you are, and into yourself, the less Satan bothers you. In other words, Satan leaves them alone for they are not doing any harm to his kingdom by seeing his children delivered from Hell and the Lake of Fire. We need to be storming the very gates of Hell to see our brothers and sisters delivered from them. LORD JESUS put the responsibility upon *our* shoulders. What do you think the great commission was about?

The closer we get in doing the will of FATHER GOD, the more interest Satan takes in our lives. The more like LORD JESUS we become, the more offensively Satan tries to make us fall through our old natures. If we are not *well* versed in dealing with our old natures, seeing them <u>dead</u>, we will be caught off guard when Satan attacks. And I say "when," because I know Satan doesn't want us becoming like LORD JESUS, and storming the gates of Hell. Satan wants all his children to share in his Eternal punishment. And he will take down anyone who isn't privy to his ways.

I believe the first thing to readjust in our walk with FATHER GOD and our LORD JESUS, *is* how we see LORD JESUS. HE *is* The KING of Kings, and The LORD of Lords. HE *is* Alpha and Omega, the beginning and the ending. REVELATION 1:5-8
Says:

> From JESUS CHRIST, *Who is* the faithful witness, *and* the first begotten from the dead, and the Prince of the kings of the earth. Unto HIM that loved us, and washed us from our sins in HIS own blood, and hath made us kings and priests unto GOD and HIS FATHER; to HIM *be* glory and dominion forever and ever. Amen. Behold, HE cometh with clouds; and every eye shall see HIM, and they *also* which pierced HIM: and all kindreds of the earth shall wail because of HIM. Even so, Amen. "I am Alpha and Omega, the beginning and the ending," saith the LORD, which is, and which was, and which is to come, the ALMIGHTY.

That verse is *awesome*! All shall see HIM, even those that pierced HIM; meaning those that drove the nails into HIS hands! LORD JESUS is it! My LORD, and Savior, my GOD, *and* my Friend and Brother; I couldn't be in better hands.

When FATHER GOD changed my prayer ending to 'in THY Name, my LORD JESUS,' it brought me so much closer to HIM. Instead of just ending the prayer by saying 'and we ask it in JESUS' Name,' even though it says in the WORD to do that, take it to the next level, by acknowledging LORD JESUS presence. After all, HE *is* sitting there at FATHER GOD's right hand! And HE is LORD over all creation, including us!

Chapter 19

I'd like to talk about a subject that is close to my heart. Actually *it is* in my heart; it's the love of LORD JESUS CHRIST. There is verse after verse describing HIS magnificent love; the epitome being that HE suffered a horrible death, after being rejected by the people HE came to save; HE carried *all* of our sins on HIS cross, and abolished the wall between our Holy Heavenly FATHER and ourselves, allowing us, HIS brethren, and sisters access to our Holy Heavenly FATHER in HIS Holy Name.

That love, which is shed abroad in our hearts, is the source of all the love we feel and have for each other, as brother and sister in our LORD JESUS. Consider this: do you think we could love each other as deeply and completely without that love? Of course not. The first and foremost commandment, "Thou shalt love the LORD thy GOD with all your heart, soul, mind and strength," and its companion, "Thou shalt love thy neighbor as thyself;" opens the door to understanding the love in our hearts for each other.

First of all, when you pray for these commandments to be manifested in your lives, I recommend that you pray that you love yourself as FATHER GOD loves you, *then* pray that you love your neighbor as yourself. That way, you know that the love you are asking for is of FATHER GOD. I often wondered about that; what if you had a very low esteem of yourself, or GOD forbid, hated yourself. You wouldn't want to love your brother and sister like you loved yourself then, would you? A lot of people are very hard on themselves, and see themselves as less than what they want or need to fulfill obligations of society, or even to their families. The need to see ourselves as FATHER GOD sees us is vital, for GOD sees us through eyes of *love*. I've learned that you can't love anyone else, if you don't love yourself.

And what of the WORD? If we are truly dead, what is there *to* love? The body we are in? Yes. It is the temple of the HOLY SPIRIT. Our soul? Yes, again. It contains our minds, emotions, feelings, our heart's desires, and really, all that we are. And most important, our spirit, which is alive only because of LORD JESUS, and what HE did when HE was raised from the dead; and what HE does, when we ask HIM into our hearts.

Loving ourselves in this manner has lead Satan to pervert what love is; causing people to worship the body; offering people the temptation of fornication in order to love ourselves in this body we are in. It all gets very complicated from here. The only way to sort it out is to go back to the WORD.

The complication begins with the varying degrees of relationships we have with the bodies we are in; for example, if we are overweight, we tend to shy away from loving the body we are in; if we are physically disabled, the same can be said. On the other hand, if we are pretty, or handsome, we tend to think too much of ourselves; pride in the body then becomes the enemy. Do you see why it is hard for us to love our neighbor as ourselves? It is much more than making sure that you have food for the body; personal hygiene and clothing for the body are merely needful requirements. The real love for the body we are in is seeing the needs of our brothers and sisters in this physical realm, and supplying them as we are able. As the WORD says:

> If a brother or sister be naked, and destitute of daily food, and one of you say unto them, depart in peace, be ye warmed and filled; notwithstanding ye give them not those things which are needful to the body; what does it profit?

> (JAMES 2:15,16.)

The love of LORD JESUS CHRIST in our hearts causes us to fulfill the commandments of FATHER GOD, in that we love ourselves, we love FATHER GOD and HIS SPIRIT and SON, and we love our neighbors, brothers, and sisters in our LORD JESUS, and filling the needs of not only the bodies we are in, but of those around us. That love should be the motivating factor behind everything we do in this body. It *will* be, when we see each other as FATHER GOD and our LORD JESUS sees us.

Chapter 20

The LORD just gave me an insight that HE wants me to share with you. As the WORD says:

> For as it is written, *As* I live, saith the LORD, every knee shall bow to ME, and every tongue shall confess to GOD.
>
> (ROMANS 14:11.)

> That at the Name of JESUS every knee should bow, of *things* in Heaven, and *things* in earth, and *things* under the earth; and *that* every tongue should confess that JESUS CHRIST *is* LORD, to the glory of GOD the FATHER.
>
> (PHILIPPIANS 2:10,11.)

As we see each other in varying degrees of popularity, with envy being present at times, even hatred towards our fellow man because of *their* popularity or prosperity, all will be as nought on the day that we stand before the LORD JESUS CHRIST. What we have to get a hold of *here*, is that we can't be partial to anyone; no respect of persons, as FATHER GOD does not. As the WORD says:

> My Brethren, have not the faith of our LORD JESUS CHRIST, *the LORD* of glory, with respect of persons. For if there come unto your assembly a man with a gold ring, in goodly apparel, and there come in also a poor man in

vile raiment; And you have respect to him that has the gay clothing, and say unto him, sit thou here in a good place; and say to the poor, stand thou there, or sit here under my footstool: Are you not then partial in yourselves, and are become judges of evil thoughts? Hearken, my beloved brethren, Hath not GOD chosen the poor of this world rich in faith, and heirs of the Kingdom, which HE has promised to them which love HIM? But you have despised the poor. Do not rich men oppress you, and draw you before the judgment seats? Do not they blaspheme that worthy Name by the which you are called? If you fulfill the royal law according to the Scripture, Thou shall love thy neighbor as thyself, you do well: but if you have respect of persons, you commit sin, and are convinced of the law as transgressors.

(JAMES 2: 1-9.)

All this WORD is a build-up to this: Hero worship, and envy of prominent people is just a way of worshipping them, even though this sounds extreme; For there is only ONE Who is worthy of worship: The FATHER, the SON, and the HOLY SPIRIT; and these are ONE. So don't say within you, "wow, *they* will bow their knee to JESUS!" As I did once; I have had respect of persons, and I regret this very much. I have hurt some people by thinking too lowly of them, just as I have hurt people by thinking too highly of them, causing pride in them.

First of all, HE is *LORD* JESUS; and second of all, no respect of persons! Love all men, and women as FATHER GOD loves them; as LORD JESUS loves them. HE gave up HIS life for them!

"Greater love hath no man than this, that a man lay down his life for his friends. You are MY friends, if you do whatsoever I command you."

(JOHN 15: 13,14.)

What exactly does it mean to love your neighbor as yourself? In any case, I take care of my needs, so I would then take care of their needs, (as much as I am able to, financially, emotionally) being a support to them in any way that I can. In other words, love in action.

If I were to analyze my relationships right now, mainly with my sons and my physical family, and my family in my LORD JESUS, I would say that my LORD has a lot of work to do in me; I try to deal with people the same way; if they have needs that I can meet, I consider the WORD:

> Withhold not good from them whom it is due, when it is in the power of thine hand to do *it*. Say not unto thy neighbor, go, and come again, and tomorrow I will give, when thou hast it by thee.

> (PROVERBS 3:27,28.)

I still deal with people considering how they have dealt with me in the past; those that I have just met, it's different. Those I love and feed as I would my Brothers and Sisters in my LORD JESUS CHRIST. Those that have wronged me in the past, or been arbitrary to what I believe and think I must consider carefully. The HOLY SPIRIT instructs me to deal with them according to the WORD. That's if I have the time to think about it. If I don't have time to consider carefully, I tend to rationalize my actions and reactions towards them by what I can get out of the situation. (What's in it for me?) This is the wrong way to think about anyone, I know.

I choose to forgive those that have wronged me in the past, for the WORD says, that my FATHER won't forgive me if I don't from my heart, forgive. But consider yourself. What do you do in a pinch? Depending upon how close you are to LORD JESUS' image, you would resort to your baser old nature reactions; unless the HOLY SPIRIT directly intervened. I have had it work both ways. I much prefer the HOLY SPIRIT's intervention. All that requires is to walk in the SPIRIT, and to live in the SPIRIT. HE will lead the situation to HIS purpose- that of glorifying the LORD JESUS and FATHER GOD. Of the multitude of good things that happen when HE does this, HE speaks through me, and the possible confrontation is disarmed. FATHER GOD and my LORD JESUS are glorified, and the person that I was at odds with is now my friend again.

What have I been saying all along? Love yourself as FATHER GOD and LORD JESUS loves you, and then love your neighbor as yourself. Love FATHER GOD with all your heart, soul, mind and strength; and if you have trouble doing any of these things, ask FATHER GOD in LORD

JESUS' Name; how much do you love me? HE will direct you back to the WORD, where it says:

> For GOD so loved the world, that HE gave HIS only begotten SON, that whosoever should believe in HIM should not perish, but have everlasting life.

> (JOHN 3:16.)

LORD JESUS loved us enough to suffer the humiliation of voluntary torture and eventual crucifixion, dying on that cross for each of us. We cannot afford to lose sight of that very important truth. ALL of our sins HE took to death with HIM on that cross. We are now HIS FATHER's Children! We are LORD JESUS' Brothers and Sisters! All because of THEIR love for us; I speak this to the Body of CHRIST; if you have read this far and are still not asking LORD JESUS into your heart, please ask now. If you don't, I fear Satan will steal the desire to away from you, and you will spend Eternity in the Lake of Fire. Don't let Satan win. The Devil doesn't love you, even though the things he tempts you with are pleasurable things. He uses these to lure you away from FATHER GOD, and to satisfy yourself. I know what that is like. No amount of pleasure or self satisfaction is worth suffering in the Lake of Fire forever! Please become my brother or sister in my LORD JESUS!

There are those that will look at my track record, and they will see hypocrisy over and over again. All can point their finger my direction; but please take the writing for what it is; The WORD doesn't change just because the one who delivers it was once lost in a sin (meaning me- and these writings) I am only writing as I am led to. Let me ask you a question; do you have a calling on your life? Wouldn't you have a hard time fulfilling it if Satan were constantly busy trying to sway you away from that calling? I am still not resistant to sin, this I admit. I have been lonely too long, seeking FATHER GOD for a mate that has not showed herself yet. I am tired, and not always ready to take the hard road. Call me a hypocrite, this I know I am; but I am trying to finish what FATHER GOD started so long ago, when I became HIS Child. If you knew what it is like having voices screaming at you, condemning you for everything you do or don't do; plus your own internal voice, guilty because of sin committed, weighing on you-you wouldn't be so eager to pounce on me. I am doing the best I know how, when at every turn there is a multitude of signs saying this is the way to go; and as many voices saying that they are the right way, most of which sounding like the HOLY SPIRIT's voice. The only way I can tell is to differentiate between what they are telling me to do. I have chosen the wrong way <u>several</u> times; and I am always drawn back to this- the calling on my life to finish these books and get them published and read by everyone that FATHER GOD has already chosen to read them.

Chapter 21

Let me tell you of a man, I do not know his name; he was told by FATHER GOD that he had a calling on his life to go out and preach. The man didn't go. Several times the LORD told him to go and preach, each time the man refused. Then one afternoon the man was lying on his couch, and he started screaming at the top of his lungs, "Help me!! I'm burning, burning in HELL!!!" His wife ran in to find him screaming, and they took him to the emergency room at the hospital, where they cut off his pants to find he had 3rd degree burns from his toes to his waist. From what the man said, he had been dipped in HELL's flames!

The man, after he had recovered from the burns, decided to go and preach, and with what a testimony! A good friend of mine told me of this man, and if the story is true, (not to question the integrity of my friend), it would mean that FATHER GOD takes serious measures to ensure that those who will come to HIS Kingdom through the preaching of a man such as this, *get* into HIS Kingdom. My point of this story is that I have been to the Lake of Fire, and still have a tendency to disobey. It doesn't help when a voice like unto the HOLY SPIRIT's voice tells me that there is a place reserved in Heaven for my dad, and one in HELL reserved for me. My mom, bless her, tells me that those voices that tell me these things are of the schizophrenic kind, and I'd like to believe her. But I know the WORD. The trouble is that I don't always obey it. The condemnation that I endure is awful, and relentless. All the while I keep going back to these books and what FATHER GOD started so long ago in me, hoping that I have not pressed HIM too far. Hoping that the next time I am tempted, I will choose the right path. Even though I know myself, and what I am capable of. I really hate that part of me that bows to sin. It is the old nature, and about it the WORD says:

But ye have not so learned CHRIST; if so be that ye
have heard HIM, and have been taught by HIM, as the
truth is in JESUS: that ye put off concerning the former
conversation the old man, which is corrupt according to
the deceitful lusts; and be renewed in the spirit of your
mind; and that ye put on the new man, which after GOD
is created in righteousness and true holiness.

(EPHESIANS 4:20-23.)

The main problem with the transformation process, (what I mean
by transformation process is old nature to new nature, from secular to
spiritual) is that Satan has planted lies saying that it is "ok" to have the old
nature along with the new nature; when the truth is, that the old nature
must die. Again, the WORD says:

I am crucified with CHRIST: nevertheless I live; yet not
I, but CHRIST liveth in me: and the life which I now live
in the flesh I live by the faith of the SON of GOD, who
loved me and gave HIMSELF for me.

(GALATIANS 2:20.)

Know ye not, that so many of us as were baptized into
JESUS CHRIST were baptized into HIS death? Therefore
we are buried with HIM by baptism into death: that like
as CHRIST was raised up from the dead by the glory of
the FATHER, even so we also should walk in newness of
life. For if we have been planted together in the likeness
of HIS death, we shall be also *in the likeness* of *HIS*
resurrection: knowing this, that our old man is crucified
with *HIM* that the body of sin might be destroyed, that
henceforth we should not serve sin. For he that is dead is
freed from sin.

(ROMANS 6: 3-7.)

And an interesting verse in MATTHEW that I have always strived to understand; it speaks of the old and new natures:

> "No man putteth a piece of new cloth unto and old garment, for that which is put in to fill up taketh from the garment, and the rent is made worse. Neither do men put new wine in old bottles: else the bottles break, and the wine runneth out, and the bottles perish: but they put new wine into new bottles, and both are preserved."

(MATTHEW 9:16,17.)

I feel like the first of these analogies describes the way I have been attempting to merge the old nature with the new nature; instead of doing it the way the WORD says to. After 28 years of life as a Christian, following my own design for how my "walk" should be, I can safely say that my LORD JESUS is now, as in "now," right at this very moment I am writing this, allowing me to "put on" the new man. All the time I have spent doing things the way that I wanted them to go, even praying for situations to be changed to satisfy my desires, I give up right now in THY Name, my LORD JESUS. I repent of seeking my own way, in order to fulfill YOUR perfect will in my life. And I praise YOU for it.

Put on the new man, the WORD says; how does one "put on" the nature of the new man? First, I believe we need to understand just what we have when we are born (as babies). We have a body, which is obvious; we have a soul, for as the WORD says:

> And the LORD GOD formed man *of* the dust of the ground, and breathed into his nostrils the breath of life; and man became a living soul.

(GENESIS 2:7.)

This soul stays with us throughout our lives, and is eternal (either Heaven or hell). The following verses describe Eternity in first hell, then the Lake of Fire:

"And fear not them which kill the body, but are not able to kill the soul: but rather fear HIM which is able to destroy both soul and body in Hell."

(MATTHEW 10:28)

And the Devil that deceived them was cast into the Lake of Fire and Brimstone, where the beast and the false prophet *are*, and shall be tormented day and night forever and ever. And I saw a great white Throne, and HIM Who sat on it, from Whose face the earth and the Heaven fled away; and there was found no place for them. And I saw the dead, small and great, stand before GOD; and the books were opened: and another book was opened, which is *the Book* of Life: and the dead were judged out of those things which were written in the books, according to their works. And the sea gave up the dead which were in it; and death and hell gave up the dead which were in them: and they were judged every man according to their works. And death and hell were cast into the Lake of Fire. This is the second death. And whosoever was not found written in the Book of Life was cast into the Lake of Fire.

(REVELATION 20:10-15.)

Chapter 22

The good part is this, as LORD JESUS said:

> "I am the resurrection and the life: he that believeth in ME, though he were dead, yet shall he live: And whosoever liveth and believeth in ME shall never die."

> (JOHN 11:25,26.)

> "For GOD so loved the world, that HE gave HIS only begotten SON, that whosoever believeth in HIM should not perish but have everlasting life."

> (JOHN 3:16)

These verses, as LORD JESUS spoke them, speak of Eternity in Heaven with HIM. When we become born again, our spirit becomes alive before FATHER GOD. The old nature is crucified, and all things begin anew.

As the WORD says:

> Therefore if any man *be* in CHRIST, *he is* a new creature: old things are passed away; behold all things are become new.

> (2nd CORINTHIANS 5:17.)

These three, (body, soul, and spirit) combined make up the vessel we know as the born again man; (or woman, as the case may be), and with

FATHER GOD and LORD JESUS and their SPIRIT inside us, we should be as the WORD says, more than conquerors:

> Who shall separate us from the love of CHRIST? Shall tribulation, or distress, or persecution, or famine, or nakedness, or peril, or sword? As it is written, For THY sake we are killed all the daylong; we are accounted as sheep for the slaughter. Nay, in all these things we are more than conquerors through HIM that loved us.

(ROMANS 8:35-37.)

The time is coming very quickly where we (the Body of CHRIST) will be put in the position where we will have to choose between Faith in our LORD JESUS, and adjusting to the world's standard of monetary commerce (the mark of the beast 666) I know that a great falling away will happen very soon, for as the WORD says:

> Let no man deceive you by any means: for *that day shall not come,* except there come a falling away first, and that man of sin be revealed, the son of perdition; who opposeth and exalteth himself above all that is called GOD, or that is worshipped; so that he as GOD sitteth in the temple of GOD, showing himself that he is GOD.

(2ⁿᵈ THESSALONIANS 2:3,4.)

Preparations for our LORD JESUS' return in our hearts and minds must include unity in the Body of CHRIST as we stand as one against those who *will* persecute us, especially when we are the only ones to refuse the mark; which will, to the lost seem like a miraculous answer to all the world's problems. We will be ridiculed, hated, and probably killed outright for our faith in our LORD JESUS CHRIST; but as LORD JESUS said:

> "Because iniquity shall abound, the love of many shall wax cold. But he that shall endure unto the end, the same shall be saved."

(MATTHEW 24:12)

Now that the LORD has written this through these hands, I stand abashed and humbled, knowing that there is <u>no time</u> for *any kind* of voluntary sinning; we must be moving straight and steadily towards becoming like our LORD JESUS. That which I found pleasurable needs to be recognized for what it is-a straight forward attack by Satan to get me to sin against my FATHER GOD thereby separating me from my LORD. Please join me now in prayer for the Body of CHRIST.

FATHER GOD, in THY Name, LORD JESUS, we come to THEE, in agreement to seek THY Face and THY Mercy upon us, as YOUR Body continues to grow and deepen in THEE. YOUR Mercy we ask for the times are getting rough, and they are about to get even rougher, what with the financial crunch, and the truth that money will soon be obsolete, and the mark of the beast put into motion. There are some contentions in THY Body LORD JESUS, about THY return. Let us be vigilant about watching and praying, as YOU instructed us to do. YOUR WORD says that no man, not even the angels of Heaven know the day or hour, but only YOU, FATHER GOD. It is our prayer that YOU would make us to be ready for THY return, LORD JESUS. Sanctify us, and prepare us for the coming tribulation, and the stand that we, as THY Body will soon have to make. Daily feed us with keeping our confidence in THEE. Strengthen us and exercise us in the faith that YOU, YOURSELF have given us, LORD JESUS. We pray for more Grace to be sufficient for us, that we would be found in THEE at all times, day or night. And mostly, we ask for YOU to take us HOME. We love THEE, and ask these things in THY Holy Name, LORD JESUS. Amen.

As LORD JESUS changes us into HIS image, one important aspect of these changes is our reactions being like HIS; reacting with love, and patience with understanding towards our fellow man, rather than judging them, and being offended; and if you think about it, if both of you do these things, there would be no offence given or taken. Understanding, and love would be the reaction between you. Wouldn't that be a change!

LORD JESUS wanted me to include in this book a description of the Lord's Prayer, verse by verse. It is from MATTHEW chapter 6, verses 7 through 13. I took it from the New King James Version:

> "And when you pray, do not use vain repetitions as the heathen *do*, for they think they shall be heard for their many words. Therefore do not be like them. For your FATHER knows the things you have need of before you ask HIM.

> In this manner, therefore, pray: Our FATHER in Heaven, Hallowed be YOUR Name.YOUR Kingdom come, YOUR will be done on earth as *it is* in Heaven.Give us this day our daily bread. And forgive us our debts, as we forgive our debtors. And do not lead us into temptation, but deliver us from the evil one.For YOURS is the Kingdom and the power and the glory forever. Amen"

There are a few additions that the King James Version brings to the Lord's Prayer, and I will expand on those in a few moments. To begin, "Our FATHER," really does say it all. GOD *is* our FATHER, both now and FOREVER! "In Heaven, hallowed be THY Name." FATHER GOD resides in Heaven, and in our hearts. HE is HOLY. Even HIS Name is HOLY, and to be worshipped and reverenced when we speak it: JEHOVAH JIREH. "YOUR Kingdom come, YOUR will be done on earth as *it is* in Heaven." As the Kingdom of GOD expands in our hearts, FATHER GOD's will *is* being done here on earth. This part of the WORD of GOD tells me that it was GOD's plan to have Lucifer found with pride. It was no mistake on GOD's part. I believe that FATHER GOD planned it to be this way, so HE would have a people who would choose HIM over sin; a peculiar people that would obey HIM, and love HIM both now, and throughout Eternity.

"Give us this day our daily bread." This is not just talking about food. In truth, our daily bread consists of everything FATHER GOD has for us in this day; from HIS loving chastisement, to the kind words that you hear from your spouse, or neighbor. The WORD, or our LORD JESUS CHRIST and the ingesting of HIM by reading the WORD is a BIG part of our daily bread. Even the hateful words that come our way through those who aren't where they should be are planned. They are meant to teach us patience and forgiveness, and understanding between each other. Praise FATHER GOD for our daily bread!

"And forgive us our debts, as we forgive our debtors." Remember the WORD. It says in MATTHEW:

> "For if you forgive men their trespasses, your Heavenly FATHER will also forgive you: but if you forgive not men their trespasses, neither will your FATHER forgive your trespasses."

> (MATTHEW 6:14,15)

This is a delusion or lie that Satan has laid upon the Body of CHRIST; that we are forgiven, when we still have unforgiveness in our hearts towards people in our lives; especially unforgiveness towards those who are not of the Body. Make sure when you pray that you are asking for any unforgiveness to be revealed by the HOLY SPIRIT. Praise GOD for the privilege of prayer. Use it to be set free. Asking is free; and as the WORD says:

...You have not because you ask not.

(JAMES 4:2.)

You ask, and receive not, because you ask amiss, that ye may consume *it* upon your lusts.

(JAMES 4:3)

"For YOURS is the Kingdom, and the power and the glory, forever. Amen."

I believe that when all LORD JESUS' enemies have been made HIS footstool, and all has been accomplished, LORD JESUS will hand over the Kingdom to HIS FATHER, and all will be in subjection to HIM for Eternity. I've been hunting the Scriptures for this, and haven't found it yet, though I remember hearing about this or reading it somewhere. At this time I don't know. I only believe it in faith.

Chapter 23

Hypocrisy is one thing I've found in Scripture that is really targeted as a reason to end up in the Lake of Fire; that, and lying. The way I see it, living hypocritically is living a lie; pretending to be spiritual when you are actually very wicked; as in the days when LORD JESUS was walking this earth, and HIS dealings with the Pharisees. They made a show of being spiritual, yet LORD JESUS knew they were hypocrites.
The WORD says:

> "Woe unto you, scribes and Pharisees, hypocrites! For you make clean the outside of the cup and of the platter, but within they are full of extortion and excess. *Thou* blind Pharisee, cleanse first that *which is* within the cup and platter, that the outside of them may be clean also."
>
> (MATTHEW 23:25,26)

> "Even so ye also outwardly appear righteous unto men, but within ye are full of hypocrisy and iniquity."
>
> (MATTHEW 23:28)

Hypocrisy in my own life has taken the form of being spiritual in front of my Christian family, and when I get around those who aren't of the Body of CHRIST, acting in accordance with their beliefs (and unbeliefs). I am getting better, though. I have been more of a witness to the power and love of my LORD JESUS in all of my life and the lives of my flock than I've ever been. I really am changing every day; changing into my

LORD JESUS' image. I am attempting to deny myself, as my LORD JESUS wants us to.

My fleshly drives are very strong, and with the schizophrenia I have, I don't always succeed. All I know is I am on *the* road to completely denying my fleshly desires. When I buckle under the tidal wave of temptation that Satan hits me with, coupled with the prideful act of disobedience of the commandments of GOD, it's usually too late to remember the WORD:

> There hath no temptation taken you but such is common to man: but GOD *is* faithful, Who will not suffer you to be tempted above that which you are able; but will with the temptation also make a way to escape, that ye may be able to bear *it*.

> (1st CORINTHIANS 10:13.)

The key to finding the escape that FATHER GOD makes for me when I am tempted, is of course to *look for it*. When I am tempted with disobedience, look for the opportunity to obey HIM.

I have a very old picture depicting LORD JESUS walking on the water, with Peter sinking into the temptuous waves, reaching out to LORD JESUS, Who has HIS hand out to save Peter. When I look upon this picture, I am reminded that Peter actually *did* walk on the water too; as long as he had his eyes and focus solely on LORD JESUS. When he started to look at the waves and the tempus around him, he began to sink. There is also the truth that LORD JESUS bid him come onto the water. When I have my eyes on my LORD JESUS, I can accomplish tremendous things-like this book. When my eyes stray away, it's like the WORD says:

> But every man is tempted, when he is drawn away of his own lust, and enticed. Then when lust hath conceived, it bringeth forth sin: and sin, when it is finished, bringeth forth death.

> (JAMES 1:14,15.)

I know the truth; Women are my sisters and my mothers, and my daughters. Those of the Body of CHRIST are my Sisters in my LORD JESUS. Today I am writing strongly in the SPIRIT; Only FATHER GOD and LORD JESUS know about tomorrow. The LORD told me once to obey HIM in secret; all I have is right now. Obedience to the WORD right now; my psycho counselors advise me to listen to my still small voice, that of the HOLY SPIRIT. They understand my spiritual values, and respect them. I listened to my still small voice yesterday, and repented of listening to the secular music I was listening to, prayed, as I was led to, and began writing, under the influence of the HOLY SPIRIT. What I wrote impressed me strongly. The impression I got was that FATHER GOD and my LORD JESUS were not mad at me; They had waited patiently for me to come back to them, by FATHER GOD's goodness; then they blessed my understanding again, allowing me to write by the direction of the HOLY SPIRIT.

Praise YOU three as ONE!

Chapter 24

LORD JESUS instructed me to write about the spoken word as I was praying this morning. It is what I want to do; please HIM with obedience to HIS direction. I have a general idea what direction I want to take with this, but that can *always* change mid stride, depending on what the HOLY SPIRIT leads; and that is who I follow. Let me begin with a verse from the WORD:

> Death and life *are* in the power of the tongue: and they that love it shall eat the fruit thereof.

> (PROVERBS 18:21.)

A close friend told me once that she was going to Hell, because of the things she does in her mind; bear in mind that this person is a Christian; and knowledgeable of the WORD. I told her seriously that she needed to quit speaking that, and confess that she is going to Heaven, and pray to FATHER GOD about her mind. I firmly believe it is within our power as humans to speak things into existence; an example-if I speak that I am depressed, over and over, guess what? I'm going to be depressed.

There are numerous factors to consider when applying this; such as, is it according to FATHER GOD's will? If we have prayed for GOD's will to be done in this earth as it is in Heaven, it will be. Prayer is *the* most powerful tool we have at our disposal for speaking things into existence. I pray every morning for the fruit of the HOLY SPIRIT to be manifested in our lives (myself and the entire Body of CHRIST, and my flock), and I believe it is being done. Faith and prayer are partners in the manifesting of the spoken word.

Another factor is confession; the WORD tells us that we must confess with our mouths:

> That if thou shalt confess with thy mouth the LORD JESUS, and shalt believe in thine heart that GOD hath raised HIM from the dead, thou shalt be saved.

> (ROMANS 10:9.)

> "Whosoever therefore shall confess ME before men, him will I confess before MY FATHER which is in Heaven. But whosoever shall deny ME before men, him will I also deny before MY FATHER which is in Heaven."

> (MATTHEW 10:32,33)

These are perfect examples of death and life in the power of confession of the mouth; the first, confessing LORD JESUS, is life, and Eternal life at that; the second, denying LORD JESUS, is death, and you guessed it, Eternal death. Another verse:

> "But I say unto you, that every idle word that men shall speak, they shall give account thereof in the Day of Judgment. For by thy words thou shalt be justified, and by thy words thou shalt be condemned."

> (MATTHEW 12:37)

Makes you want to watch what you say, doesn't it? I sincerely hope so. And I pray so, for you who are reading this right now, in my LORD JESUS' Name. Here is more of the WORD to consider:

> "...For out of the abundance of the heart, the mouth speaketh."

> (MATTHEW 12:34)

This tells me that if I want to speak life, my heart must be right with FATHER GOD. Again, confession of my mouth, my sins, I know that LORD JESUS is just and faithful to forgive them, and cleanse me from all unrighteousness, making my heart clean and ready to speak life.

I know that the whole idle words thing bothers me, and it must bother you, if you think about it. How do we communicate problems to others, if we are afraid of speaking idly? How do we start conversations, and even carry on a conversation, without it being idle? Think of it as a car; a vehicle that is idling, is in neutral; conversations that are idle are neutral in content. Our direction in conversation needs to always be toward Heavenly things:

> Only let your conversation be as it becometh the Gospel...
>
> (PHILIPPIANS 1:27.)

> For our conversation is in Heaven; from whence also we look for the Saviour, the LORD JESUS CHRIST...
>
> (PHILIPPIANS 3:20.)

> Let no corrupt communication proceed out of your mouth, but that which is good to use of edifying, that it may minister grace unto the hearers.
>
> (EPHESIANS 4:29.)

I've been watching my words lately, seeing how difficult it really is to only speak about Heavenly things. I don't want to advise you on how to carry on conversations, if I am not willing to do what I advise.

One time I was outside talking BS with some friends of mine. They started talking about body piercings- you know, nose, tongue etc; I didn't join in on the conversation, not having any of my own; later I was told what I should have been talking about- LORD JESUS' body piercings, and carried the conversation to HIS sacrifice. It would have been apples of gold in pictures of silver. I wouldn't have been scared to talk, if I knew beforehand that the conversation was going to end up in that way.

In this case, silence was deadly, robbing those who were listening of a perfect witness, and quite possibly, the only one they will hear from me; unless I pray for another opening to speak life for them. That depends on how much I really, truly love them as my brothers, and want them to know my LORD JESUS. And as we know, it's not just to know LORD JESUS; it's saving them from the Lake of Fire Eternally. Selfish indifference then becomes my enemy. As you can probably tell, I'm fighting with this one at this very moment; and I will win. I will continue to pray for them, and pray for another opportunity to share with them the wonderful truth of the Gospel, with apples of gold in pictures of silver again.

After being led to ask for what to do at this very moment, I am told that I need to write about my daily life now, as concerning the sanctification process in my life. So here goes:

As purposed in my first book, CHOSEN VESSEL, I begin the day by greeting my Holy Heavenly FATHER and my LORD JESUS, and their HOLY SPIRIT, thanking them for getting me through another night of very realistic dreams; I believe the first person I should talk to is the One who gives me life once again this morning.

To you who have spouses, you might want to slip into your private room that only FATHER GOD sees you in, and bid them good morning. That's if you feel uncomfortable doing that in front of your spouse. The ideal thing, and that which I am looking for, is to be with a woman who delights in sharing my relationship with my LORD and FATHER; one who respects the truth that they are my first love; my spouse comes second to my relationship with them. She knows that all my heart loves her, and that love is in my LORD JESUS.

After bidding them good morning, I start to pray for the Body of CHRIST, myself, and my flock included. Again, ideally, I will have my spouse pray along side of me holding my hand before FATHER GOD. I am led for what to pray, by my LORD JESUS; and if I can't remember what to ask for, the HOLY SPIRIT reminds me (that still amazes me that they talk to me- they truly are closer than my own breath), which took some getting used to- the truth that they listen to and hear everything; even what my heart meditates on. They see everything that plays in the screen of my mind, and advise me when it gets to sinning by leading me to repentance, forgiving me immediately when I ask them for forgiveness. I can't imagine what it's like to know *everything* continually; to see everything continually. How big our GOD *is*; the truths that HE is everywhere, and every when… just blows the roof off my imagination.

Chapter 25

I tend to think of GOD as an old, wizened man sitting on HIS Throne; probably because I've seen pictures depicting HIM in that way. I hate preconceived ideas. I want to see HIM as HE *is*; mighty, with terrible majesty before HIM; lightening flashing, claps of deafening thunder before HIM reacting to HIS righteous judgments on earth. I want my conception of FATHER GOD and my LORD JESUS to be beyond my wildest true imaginations; those given by the WORD itself, and what I've already been shown in the SPIRIT.

Beside them there is no other; my LORD and FATHER, their Mercy in my life has been above and beyond what any mortal man should have to be given. Their Grace, oh their Grace…unwarranted favor, as I've heard it described; the only way I have survived so far. It is how I keep praying each morning. Mercy and Grace, and their Love intertwined with the faith that my LORD JESUS has given me, being the Author and Finisher of my faith; that's how I am still on this road to sanctification.

Speaking of being on the road to sanctification, if you have read my first book, CHOSEN VESSEL, you know that I have an acute case of schizophrenia. I asked the LORD what HE wanted me to write about this evening. HE then told me to write about how my illness affects the sanctification process in my life, and vice versa, meaning how the sanctification process affects my condition of schizophrenia. This is somewhat complicated, so bear with me as I succeed in telling about this.

I cannot separate my spiritual life from my everyday life, any more than I can separate the schizophrenia from my everyday life. It comes as a package deal. My path to sanctification affects all aspects of my life, including my mental condition. Please allow me to explain.

The removal of sin patterns in my life (the basic first ingredient to sanctification) caused my schizophrenia to ease somewhat over the last few months. When I *would* sin, the stress of carrying the weight of that sin, no matter if it was just a few moments (then seeking forgiveness of my LORD JESUS) caused my symptoms to worsen; not to mention the sin itself affecting this body, my mind, and heart, and ultimately my soul.

Stress of any kind makes my symptoms get worse, and as I realize this, I am praying for FATHER GOD and my LORD JESUS to rid me of anything that does not coincide with The WORD.

I know one thing that is difficult to take about this sanctification process, the process of changing me into my LORD JESUS' image lets me know that the schizophrenia is not compatible with the mind of CHRIST. My delusional thinking patterns (aside from what is written in this book-you might be thinking that I don't show any symptoms of schizophrenia, or delusional thinking as far as what is written in this book, but I remind you that LORD JESUS is helping to write this book, by leading through the HOLY SPIRIT. When I feel the need to stop writing, due to attacks from the schizophrenia, I do so. The most evident effect of my condition would be the pattern of thought, or the thought train; the smoothness of my writing, which is evident here.

Changing my mind into the mind of CHRIST requires, of course, exposure to the WORD of GOD; reading it, to absorb it into my spirit, first of all; then for me, to read it aloud gets it into my mind, and by thinking about, meditating upon the WORD.

Chapter 26

To continue with my day- the prayers led by my LORD JESUS include asking that none of my flock, nor any of the Body of CHRIST, nor myself would receive the mark of the Beast, as it is represented- 666, of the which we will all find out soon enough what that will be. All I know is that the LORD told me my flock would be saved (Praise GOD), and that I pray those who will fall away in these last days before our LORD's return, that none of my flock, including myself would be of that group of people.

My prayers include praying for those already saved, and those who will *be* in faith saved before our LORD's return, salvation, sanctification, redemption, and repentance as it applies to each. I pray that we would all come into the unity of the faith, and of the knowledge of the SON of GOD, unto a perfect man, unto the measure of the stature of the fullness of CHRIST (EPHESIANS 4:13); and to know HIS love, which passes knowledge, and to be filled with all the fullness of GOD (EPHESIANS 3:19). That we would trust in our LORD JESUS with all our hearts, and not lean on our own understanding: acknowledging HIM in all our ways, that HE would direct our paths (PROVERBS 3:5,6).

All of my prayers take me about a half of an hour; regardless of who is already awake, I will tell them that I have to make sure of FATHER GOD's blessing on the day at hand, and go ahead and pray in my LORD JESUS' Name.

One of my most necessitated prayers involves the car in which I drive. I pray fervently that there would be no accidents, and no stopping by any law enforcement agencies for any reason, that there would be no reason to stop me- obeying the traffic rules and regulations to the letter. All this FATHER GOD grants on a daily basis, except for a day that I disobeyed HIM, and HE caused the accident I mentioned before.

I firmly believe that if we would humble ourselves and pray, we would have far fewer accidents and traffic tickets, because what changes when I pray these things is me. FATHER GOD has me driving the speed limit, not running traffic lights, etc. and if I ever do get a ticket, it will be because I wasn't listening, and obeying HIM at the time I was stopped. I have actually been shown what could have happened, had I not prayed for FATHER GOD's intervention. Seeing close call accidents, which I praise HIM for thwarting; seeing law enforcement radar traps that I would have been caught, had I not prayed.

I was just reminded of another accident that I had, where I had done wrong in FATHER GOD's eyes: false witnessing in front of one of my son's friends. I was taking them home after staying the night with us, and we were listening to Christian music on my car stereo. I decided it was enough of the Christian music and put on the radio, on a secular station. Right about then, a possum came out from the side of the road; I swerved to avoid it, and ran off the side of the road, damaging my rear passenger tire. Of course, it was night time, and I thought I had to fix the flat in the dark. But LORD JESUS' Mercy had me to check the emergency kit I had in the trunk, where there was a flashlight, (With new batteries). All went well after that.

Now I know what you are probably thinking; coincidence or that FATHER GOD doesn't do things like that to HIS Children. But I'm telling you, GOD reacts to what we do in this life with HIS righteous judgments; and it was done in love, for it could have been much worse, yet still taught me the lesson quite well. FATHER GOD and our LORD JESUS *are* present!

Chapter 27

Angels. Our angels; those to whom it is given the task of getting us from point A, our birth, to rebirth into the Kingdom of our LORD JESUS, to point B, death, or the resurrection where LORD JESUS takes us Home. I believe angels exist, not only because the WORD talks about them, but because of eye catching examples from my own life, and some of my closest friends. But first, let's lay the ground work for our belief in angels:

> But to which of the angels said HE at any time, Sit on MY right hand, until I make THINE enemies THY footstool? Are they not all ministering spirits, sent forth to minister for them who shall be heirs of salvation?
>
> (HEBREWS 1:13,14.)

If you have read my previous book, CHOSEN VESSEL, you are aware of my visitation of my own angel, who helped me establish my household by giving me food, and the bear blanket which is on the cover of the book.

Angels can take the guise of any one, which is why the WORD says to be careful to entertain strangers, for some have entertained angels unawares (HEBREWS 13:2). Have you ever had a run in with an individual that just seemed to be perfect for the situation you were in? It was probably an angel you encountered. I feel sorry for what my angel has had to put up with in dealing with me. I love my LORD JESUS for my angel and his patience with me, as LORD JESUS changes me into HIS image.

I know that angels have kept me from having car accidents before; it seems they ride shotgun inside and outside my car. If everyone prayed for an angelic hedge around their cars, I believe at least all those who prayed would be protected from accidents. As I have said before, I pray this- no accidents each morning; I have seen accidents prevented by what has to be angelic activity.

I have prayed that I would see angels as they are, in my room at night; so far, nothing. But then I have the faith to move mountains right now; I can believe for any number of things to happen; the LORD just doesn't want me to see them in person, yet. Know they are there for you, given by our LORD JESUS; and it will be your own personal angel who takes you to meet the LORD in the air upon HIS glorious return.

Chapter 28

But they that wait upon the LORD shall renew *their* strength; they shall mount up with wings as eagles; they shall run, and not be weary; *and* they shall walk, and not faint.

(ISAIAH 40:31.)

My life has been a series of waiting engagements, waiting upon FATHER GOD and my LORD JESUS both for strength, and wisdom, and understanding, and especially for love; love for my fellow man, my fellow Christians, and for myself. I have waited upon them for the understanding of what THEIR holy perfect will for my life was, and is; and am just now getting to the juicy parts, where I am enjoying every moment of what they have had me waiting upon THEM for. Life *is* good. That's not to say that I haven't grumbled about having to wait; I don't think *anybody* likes waiting for that which they know the LORD has for them. But I have gotten over the hurdle of the worst part of waiting, and now see light at the end of the tunnel.

I have been asking for wisdom, and believe I am receiving it; waiting patiently as the lessons of fearing the LORD come my way.

The fear of the LORD *is* the instruction of wisdom; and before honor *is* humility.

(PROVERBS 15:33.)

To be wise is to fear the LORD, and depart from evil. I still don't walk in the fear of the LORD at all times like I'd like to; like I *will* when the WORD is manifested in my life wholly, which I am waiting upon FATHER GOD to do. As it is now, I choose to depart from that which will end me up in trouble, as do most; the closer I get to doing the will of GOD, the more I *want* to walk in HIS fear.

> When wisdom entereth into thine heart, and knowledge is pleasant to thy soul; discretion shall preserve thee, understanding shall keep thee...

> (PROVERBS 2:10.11.)

I love the WORD! Obeying it has saved me more than once. Fearing FATHER GOD, and choosing to walk in HIS fear, knowing what HE has the power to do, is only secondary to the love I feel for HIM, and HIS SON, and THEIR SPIRIT.

> Happy *is* the man *that* findeth wisdom, and the man *that* getteth understanding.

> (PROVERBS 3:13.)

And of wisdom:

> She *is* a tree of life to them that lay a hold upon her: and happy *is every one* that retaineth her. The LORD by wisdom hath founded the earth; by understanding hath HE established the heavens.

> (PROVERBS 3:18)

Patience has everything to do with waiting upon the LORD. It's by far worse if you know what you are waiting for, and have to wait. I believe being patient and waiting on the LORD glorifies HIM; Therefore I am willing to do it for HIM; my LORD told me once that HE was going to tell me what was going to happen in my life before it happened, just so I couldn't say I had anything to do with bringing it about. So far HE has been right on target and I don't foresee this changing. I've known several things were going to take place in my life before they did, and now I am about to see the manifestation of one that has been my heart's desire for going on 27 years now. PRAISE GOD!

The long years of waiting, always wondering when, and how have been the worst to endure; but one thing I can tell you for sure, is that my love for FATHER GOD and my LORD JESUS has been increased by an hundred fold knowing that THEY have had my best in mind all this time.

The LORD once told me that I would be full of the HOLY SPIRIT, and of faith; I know that faith has had a major part in how I have been waiting upon FATHER GOD. The writing of my first book, and the one you are holding right now, are part of GOD's holy perfect will for my life.

"In your patience possess ye your souls."

(LUKE 21:19.)

I believe the ultimate act of patience is that of waiting patiently for our LORD JESUS' return; not giving in to the pressure of temptation, or complacency (saying within yourselves- I don't need to get ready yet; there's plenty of time). I am asking to be changed into that which is ready *all* the time. That's the reason the LORD wanted this book written- to be an instrument in the preparation of the Body of CHRIST for HIS return.

All excitement about a soul-mate aside, my main excitement and anticipation is for the beginning of Eternity with my LORD JESUS in Heaven, either by HIS return, or my death, whichever comes first.

"And there shall be signs in the sun, and in the moon, and in the stars; and upon the earth distress of nations, with perplexity; the sea and waves roaring; men's hearts failing them for fear, and for looking after those things which are coming on the earth: for the powers of heaven shall be shaken. And then shall they see the SON of man coming in a cloud with power and great glory. And when these things begin to come to pass, then look up, and lift up your heads; for your redemption draweth nigh."

(LUKE 21:25-28)

How would you live *right now* if you <u>knew</u> LORD JESUS was coming back tomorrow? What would you do? What would you change, and why? What if HE comes back tonight? How would HE find you? In faith, waiting and watching; looking for HIM?

Prayer is the lifeline between FATHER GOD and us. Saying prayers in THY Name, LORD JESUS, brings us closer to the one we are waiting and watching for. I have asked that I would be in prayer with HIM at HIS return. Won't that be fantastic? I'll be talking to HIM, and the next second HE says to me, Kelly! It's time! There is nothing I want more than to be found ready at my LORD JESUS' return. I want to hear FATHER GOD's trumpet sound, and rejoice at my LORD's shout of acclamation, as all the angels of Heaven gather us together to meet LORD JESUS in the air!